The Financial Post

MONEY MANAGEMENT BOOK

EDITED BY ROBERT L. PERRY

a Financial Post book

Maclean-Hunter Limited

ISBN 0-88896-046-8

Printed and bound in Canada

"Let us all be happy, and live within our means, even if we have to borrer money to do it with."

Artemus Ward

Contents

The contributors

The following researched and wrote the original material on which this book is based. In one form or another, all of the chapters of the text appeared recently in The Financial Post or The Financial Post Magazine.

Sherry Boeckh, a business writer based in Toronto: chapters 13 and 21.

Anne Bower, economist on the Toronto staff of The Financial Post: chapter 1.

Peter Brimelow, on the Toronto staff of The Financial Post: chapter 20.

Robert H. Catherwood, a senior editor of The Financial Post: chapter 12.

Arnold Edinborough, author, scholar, art specialist, columnist for the Financial Post: chapters 14, 15, 17 and 18.

Raoul Engel, formerly on the staff of The Financial Post, later a broadcaster on the Global Television Network: chapter 10.

Pat Fillmore, a freelance writer based in Toronto: chapter 19.

Michael Jameson, a Toronto lawyer: chapter 11.

Wayne Lilley, on the staff of The Financial Post Magazine: chapter 8.

Dennis Mellersh, editor of Canadian Jeweller: chapter 9.

Ann Rhodes, editor of The Financial Post Magazine: chapter 16.

R. Alastair Rickard, marketing services officer, Mutual Life Assurance Co. of Canada: chapter 4.

Mark Ricketts, real estate and property editor on the Toronto staff of The Financial Post: chapters 5, 23 and 24.

Beatrice Riddell, a senior editor of The Financial Post: chapters 2, 3, 6, 7 and 22.

John M. Riley, superintendent of estate planning, Mutual Life Assurance Co. of Canada: chapter 4.

John Rolfe, on the Ottawa staff of The Financial Post: chapter 18.

Frederic Wagniere, on the Toronto staff of The Financial Post: chapter 20.

Robert L. Perry is the editor of Financial Post Books.

Introduction

This book is our latest response to requests from readers who've been following The Financial Post's continuing coverage of personal money matters. "I find your articles in layman's language very interesting and informative. The only problem is trying to file such useful information for future reference. Do you have such laymen's information available in book form?" one subscriber wrote recently, and his query was typical.

Judging from letters like that and other feedback to our editors, staff writers and executives, we've concluded that interest in the field of personal money management has grown substantially during the 1970s. More Canadians, men and women in all walks of life, are looking for more ways to save and multiply their dollars — or to have some expensive fun at no cost or low cost.

A writer working in this area can expect an almost continuous reaction from readers. The most popular titles on the sales list of Financial Post Books deal with various facets of personal money management (they're listed on the back pages), and some of them have gone into second editions and multiple printings.

There are some good reasons for all this. The overhaul of the Canadian income-tax system during the early 1970s spawned a number of schemes to encourage saving — under extremely complicated rules. The imposition of a capital-gains tax had its effect on attitudes toward the stock market relative to prime-residence real estate. The federal government dropped out of the estate-duty field, creating provincial death-tax havens right within Canada. Rising incomes and expanding leisure time have enabled more Canadians to cater to wider interests. Horse breeding is no longer the domain of the very wealthy; today a school teacher can own and fly his own plane — and sometimes make a profit doing it.

There are negative factors involved too, as most of us know

well. The stock market has been erratic. Inflation has ravaged many fixed-interest and salary incomes. There's a spooky fear of the future, a sense of loss of control, of not really understanding what's happening to the world. Quite naturally, our attention tends to swing to the ageless tangibles, real estate, gold, gems, antiques, art and so on. We're concerned about the fate that retirement will impose.

So, the pages that follow carry selections on a wide variety of money matters in which Canadians have demonstrated an interest. These pages don't spell out a total money-management program or strategy for the reader. First off, that's a highly individual matter that falls outside the scope of this book. Secondly, the purpose here is to *add* to the stock of useful information in book form, not to duplicate already-published information.

For example, these pages don't deal with familiar "paper" investments such as stocks and bonds, except in passing. That large and complex area requires — and *has* — a whole Financial Post book to itself. The coverage here of certain aspects of real estate is thin, for the same reason. The discussion on gold, also the subject of many large volumes, has been limited.

On the other hand, there are a number of chapters on various forms of registered savings plans. These nest egg/tax shelters have an enormous appeal for many Canadians, but the rules are tricky, little understood and very lightly covered (if at all) in other books. The material on mortgages, annuities, offbeat hobby-investments and tax-loss selling has been included for the same reason.

One final point. The information in this book was accurate and up-to-date as it went to press in the early spring of 1976, but law, and particularly tax law, can change rapidly and unexpectedly. Almost every time the federal government or a province brings down a new budget, it wreaks change somewhere in the tax system. Readers are urged to check with specialist advisers before making final decisions about some of the complex matters covered here.

R.L.P.

1

You vs inflation:
about keeping score

Inflation and the tax man work in mysterious ways — to the point where many income-earners simply don't know whether they're better off or worse off than they were, say, five years before.

A look at a special set of our calculations might be just what it takes to brighten your day. On the other hand, it could set you to cursing the federal Anti-Inflation Board and its income controls.

Our analysis of how taxpayers at various income levels have fared, in real terms, between 1970 and 1975, shows up some remarkably divergent trends.

— The tax system, contrary to popular belief, doesn't always work against the taxpayer, adding to the burden already imposed by inflation.

Take, for instance, a married man with two children, earning $6,600 in 1970. That was the then-current industrial composite average earnings figure (not entirely comprehensive or unambiguous, but probably the best measure available of average earnings across the economy).

A family man at that income level would have had the same after-tax purchasing power in 1975 as he'd had in 1970, if his income had risen by 34.4% over 1970's — to $8,873. What he'd needed, in short, to maintain his family's 1970 lifestyle was an increase in income between 1970 and 1975 that was considerably below the estimated 41.6% increase in the consumer price index.

Indexing of the tax system for inflation, which began in 1974, increased family allowances, and tax cuts in particular are factors in this result. (More about income-tax indexing in another chapter.)

At higher levels of income, the conventional wisdom of a tax bite that has increased the hurt done by inflation is supported by the facts — but possibly to a smaller extent than imagined. The $50,000-a-year married man in 1970 needed an income in 1975 of $72,114 (up by 44.2% from 1970) to stay even. (If tax indexing had been in effect for the full five years, the salary increase needed to stay even would have been roughly in line with inflation rather than above it.)

— The average income-earner may be better off than he sometimes feels he is. According to the Conference Board in Canada, the industrial composite of average weekly earnings increased by an estimated 14% in 1975 to average $203 (about $10,560 on an annual basis). This would have made for a total increase since 1970 of 60% in earnings, and it would have given the "average" married man a take-home income that was up by 14.6% in real terms from 1970's.

At higher levels of income, that same 60% increase in income would have been translated into a smaller percentage gain in real purchasing power — an increase, for instance, of 7.7% in the case of the family man earning $50,000 in 1970. Still, that was an increase of more than $2,000 in terms of 1970 spending power and on a dollar basis at any rate, well ahead of the gain of $850 for that "average" employee who earned $6,600 in 1970.

Take a look at your own situation in the guide on the opposite page. Then rejoice — or curse.

Assess your real financial position

Deciding whether your salary increases in recent years added up to real gains isn't easy, given the mercurial rise in inflation and the shifting tax load. This is a guide to whether you were better off in 1975 than you'd been five years before.*

Are you really ahead of where you were? Suppose you were getting this salary in 1970:	To have the same after-tax purchasing power, you'd have needed this salary in 1975:
$50,000	$72,114
$45,000	$65,119
$40,000	$57,662
$35,000	$49,852
$30,000	$42,858
$25,000	$35,465
$20,000	$28,550
$15,000	$21,544
$10,000	$14,011
$ 6,600	$ 8,873

(If you're in a tax bracket not subject to a surcharge, you can calculate your own current after-tax situation, using your payday income-tax deductions and the consumer price index.)

*Standard deductions for married man under 65 with two children under 16; all income from salary or wages; family allowances and deductions for unemployment insurance and the Canada Pension Plan are taken into account in determining "take-home" income; no allowance is made for the effect of company pension plans, RRSPs, Rhosps, provincial tax credit adjustments, etc.; tax used in the calculations is the combined federal and provincial rate applicable in the spring of 1975 in B.C. and Ontario; inflation is measured by the increase in the consumer price index (1975 estimate: 10.1%; increase from 1970 to 1975: +41.6%); in 1970, the industrial composite of average weekly wages and salaries was $126.82 (about $6,600 on an annual basis). Average weekly earnings in 1975 were estimated at $203 (about $10,560 on an annual basis).

2

Tax gimmicks, yes . . . but opportunity for you

Few would argue against the desirability of encouraging individual Canadians to save and invest. And a tax break often provides the best incentive. But in the scramble to achieve a variety of economic objectives here, or correct some inequities there, the Canadian tax system is becoming cluttered with complexities and loopholes that in the end may do more harm than the good they were intended to achieve. Take just three personal tax measures covered in this book.

— The exemption for up to $1,000 of interest/dividend income has been changed, to some extent, from a measure originally designed to encourage and protect savings into what appears to be an open invitation to borrow for the purpose of reducing income tax. Under an amendment introduced in 1975, an individual can deduct the income (up to the $1,000 limit) as well as the cost of borrowing the money to produce the income. Originally, only *net* interest or dividend income (income minus deductible borrowing expenses) qualified.

The change was made because the original formula seemed to put some taxpayers — unincorporated businessmen, farmers, investors in rental real estate — at an unfair disadvantage. Their business borrowings would have rendered them ineligible for the $1,000 investment exemption. Unfortunately it opens the gates to a flood of other taxpayers seeking to take advantage of the double exemption. The amendment has, in principle, reduced the force of the tax move as an incentive to save. There's less point in saving if you can get a tax break merely by borrowing and claiming both deductions.

— The spousal RRSP* has its gimmicks, too. Although it has the reasonable objective of encouraging one spouse to establish a retirement savings plan for the other, this measure could clearly be used for the purpose of current income-splitting. The heavily taxed spouse, say the husband, claims a tax deduction for contributions to his lightly taxed wife's RRSP. She later withdraws the money to spend. She pays tax on the money withdrawn, but at a much lower rate than her husband would have paid on the same income. (It would be wise to wait a while before terminating such a plan, or Revenue Canada might consider it an "artificial transaction.")

— The Rhosp* also, lends itself to uses for which it surely wasn't intended. Designed to encourage young couples to save to buy their homes, it also seems to encourage the shifting of the family home from one spouse to another and then back again so that each could, in turn, have a once-in-a-lifetime Rhosp. It could well be worthwhile, since if the money from a Rhosp is used to buy the house from the other spouse, or for furnishings, it will have escaped tax altogether.

"Gimmicks like these add up to bad tax policy," says Robert D. Brown, senior tax partner for Price Waterhouse & Co. and one of Canada's most respected tax authorities. "They favor the nimble and adventurous while discriminating against the unsophisticated and those without professional tax advice."

Even reasonably sophisticated individuals frequently find they haven't time to sort out all the tax-dodging possibilities today. Nor should they be expected to. What much of the gimmickry amounts to is a tax reduction for middle-income earners. But if that's what was intended, why not achieve this by way of a rate reduction? If it were meant to encourage investment, it could have been done without this kind of confusion.

The controversial interest/dividend exemption literally invites

---

*The short form used throughout this book for the Registered Retirement Savings Plan and the Registered Home Ownership Savings Plan, respectively.

taxpayers to borrow money simply to reduce income taxes. Originally, up to $1,000 of interest income from Canadian investments, *less* the taxpayer's deductible interest expense claimed for the year, had been exempt from tax. Now, up to $1,000 of interest or dividend income is eligible for the exemption, and is *not* reduced by interest expense. Clearly, it could be advantageous to borrow money to buy the interest-bearing securities, although the situation isn't as simple as that in practice.

How much advantage has, in practice, been taken of the gimmick still remains to be seen. The trend of interest rates will probably have some bearing on what happens in the future.

Here, in theory, is how it would work assuming you are borrowing to produce interest income: Suppose you borrow $10,000 at 10% (or $1,000 interest per annum) and invest it to earn 10¼% ($1,025). Your after-tax net income on this transaction would be many times the $25 ($1,025-$1,000) pre-tax net income. It would range from about $395 if your taxable income from all other sources is $15,000 to $622 if taxable income is around $75,000. That assumes federal and provincial rates applicable in B.C. and Ontario in 1975. Rates vary from province to province.

The big increase in after-tax income is because the $1,000 of interest expense as well as $1,000 of the $1,025 interest income would be deductible for tax purposes. At least the interest expense would be deductible if it could be shown it was incurred for the purpose of producing income. Hence the importance of ensuring that the interest income is slightly more than the interest expense.

Borrowing to invest in dividend-paying stocks also could be attractive — particularly considering the additional possibility of capital gain. Even without the double-exemptions introduced in 1975, the exercise of borrowing to buy dividend-paying stocks had been attractive. This is because since 1972 you've been able to calculate the dividend tax credit on the gross dividend — that is, on the "taxable amount of dividend" which is actual dividend plus one third. Under the old law in force prior to 1972, the credit was calculated on the net dividend — actual dividend minus deductible carrying charges. In addition, Revenue Canada has generally allowed the deduction of borrowing charges even where these exceed common stock dividend income — on the ground that dividend income could increase in the future.

12

It still remains to be seen, of course, how Revenue Canada will react if there's a substantial increase in claims for the interest deduction. But at least some observers doubt the government will change posture — in part because the government seems anxious to encourage investment in the stock market. Besides it could be very difficult in practice for the tax assessor to match borrowings and investment in large portfolios where transactions take place frequently.

Even though borrowing costs exceed dividend income — which would generally be the case — the after-tax income from dividends can still be respectable. Assume, for instance, that you borrow $15,000 at 10% to buy XYZ common stock yielding 6%. Borrowing costs would be $1,500 a year, dividend income $900. Pre-tax net loss would be $600. However, if taxable income from other sources in 1975 had been $15,000, the after-tax income would be $188 (in Ontario or B.C. in 1975). It would rise through the various tax levels to about $510 around the $75,000 mark.

Take a look at your own particular situation to see what use you might make of the rule — if you chose to use the gimmick.

Many observers admit there could have been inequities for farmers and unincorporated businessmen if they'd been denied the $1,000 income exemption. But in helping them, it seems that at least part of the original purpose is lost. The exemption (initially to apply to interest income only) was first proposed in 1974 as a measure to encourage and protect savings. It was expanded in 1975 to include dividend income for 1975 and subsequent years. However, there may be less incentive to save and there may be no true capital to protect — if it's all borrowed and has to be repaid.

3

Savings cum tax shelter: how the RRSP rules work

It would be hard to miss the fact that January and February have become the annual Registered Retirement Savings Plan selling season — or that RRSPs, as the plans are called, offer attractive savings and tax features. Super-intense promotion by life insurance and trust companies, banks, mutual funds, credit unions, and caisses populaires certainly keep RRSPs before the public in the weeks prior to the income-tax deadline.

In or out of season, there's a wide variety of plans on the market. You can buy RRSP funds invested in bonds, stocks, mortgages, or a combination of these securities. Or you can, if you like, administer your own RRSP, making all the investment decisions yourself. In that case, a trust company acts as trustee — for a fee. And fast-growing in popularity are group RRSPs — set up by professional or employee groups and offering some administrative cost savings. The plethora of plans make the choice of your own plan very important — and ever more difficult.

Although the RRSP has been around since 1957, its savings and tax-relief features have been broadened in recent years. And its popularity has grown accordingly.

Nevertheless, the rules are still not as well understood as they might be. For one thing, they keep changing. Not long ago, some fundamental changes were made in the Income Tax Act — changes that substantially enhanced the potential for saving for retirement. The two most important were introduction of the spousal RRSP and the $1,000 exemption for pension income. There have been subsequent changes, too, although the most recent ones are generally restrictive. Changes made in 1975, for example, removed unusual — and higher — contribution limits in certain situations where an individual is a member of a company pension plan.

It all means that careful planning is important in maximizing retirement income and reducing current tax payable.

The deadline for making an RRSP contribution that will reduce the previous year's income for tax purposes is 60 days after yearend. That means March 1, except in a leap year when it's Feb. 29. (In 1976, since Feb. 29 fell on a nonbusiness day, the deadline was extended to March 1.)

Here, in brief, are some of the tax-related savings possibilities you should keep in mind while considering an RRSP contribution:

— The spousal RRSP. You may make all or part of your annual contribution to an RRSP for your spouse and claim a deduction from your own income. There's no income restriction or requirement so far as the spouse is concerned, but the amount put into both plans may not exceed your regular annual contribution limit.

The important feature of the spousal RRSP is that income earned by the fund is attributed to the recipient spouse and is not attributed for tax purposes back to the contributor — as is generally the case when money is transferred to one spouse from another. Remember, though, the spousal plan becomes the property of your spouse and cannot be claimed by you in the event of a marriage breakdown.

— The $1,000 of annual pension-income exemption includes annuities from RRSPs providing the recipient is 65 years of age. This enhances the spousal RRSP substantially.

Taken together, the spousal RRSP and the $1,000 of pension exemption enables a retired couple to split retirement income and claim two pension exemptions — even if one spouse would not otherwise have any income but Old Age Security. (Old Age Security doesn't qualify on its own for the $1,000 pension exemption, although payments may be made eligible by transferring them into an RRSP. That can be done up to the age of 71.)

While income is split, so is tax on that income. And the combined after-tax income may be considerably more than it would have been from just one RRSP fund. (See the accompanying example.)

It depends on a variety of circumstances whether a spousal RRSP makes sense, and if so, how contributions should be divided between the contributor and his/her spouse.

Each partner's present and future income — and tax rate — must obviously be taken into consideration. So must other retirement savings programs such as company pension plans. If there is a choice between making an additional, voluntary contribution to a company plan and putting it into a spousal RRSP, the latter may be more advantageous.

In any case most married couples should examine this savings opportunity carefully and should ensure that each partner will have a pension of at least $1,000.

The spousal RRSP has been touted as a means of splitting-current income, too. The spouse with the higher tax rate (say, the husband) establishes a fund for his spouse, who in turn terminates it and pays tax on the money at her lower rate. He meanwhile, has claimed a deduction for the contribution. But that game could be dangerous. Revenue Canada has made it clear it will not look kindly on a plan that is terminated shortly after it is established, unless it can be clearly demonstrated that withdrawal of the money is prompted by genuine — and previously unexpected — need.

The department has been considering applying a section of the Income Tax Act dealing with "artificial transactions" to blatant cases of terminating spousal RRSPs. The relevant section reads this way: "In computing income for the purpose of this act, no deduction may be made in respect of a disbursement or expense made or incurred in respect of a transaction or operation that, if allowed, would unduly or artificially reduce the income."

— The Registered Home Ownership Savings Plan (called a Rhosp) should be considered in conjunction with contributions to an RRSP — providing, that is, you are eligible to have a Rhosp.

An individual may contribute up to $1,000 a year (lifetime limit of $10,000) to a Rhosp in any year in which he doesn't own an interest in residential real property. Providing money withdrawn is put into an owner-occupied house or used to purchase eligible furnishings for your own or your spouse's house, the fund and accumulated income escapes tax altogether. Otherwise, it can be rolled tax-free into an RRSP for a deferral of tax.

Contribution to a Rhosp (the deadline for the previous tax year is the same as for an RRSP) does not affect RRSP contribution limits. The Rhosp rules are not as simple as they seem at first glance and care should be taken before investing in one of these plans. (A subsequent chapter will describe the Rhosp in more detail.) But if you are eligible for a Rhosp, you should certainly consider it along with an RRSP.

— If you have unusually large amounts of specified income (such as capital gains, income received as an entertainer, or income from producing an artistic or literary work), you may want to consider deferring tax through an Income Averaging Annuity Contract (IAAC). The deadline for applying an IAAC to the previous tax year is also usually March 1, and one of these plans might provide additional tax deferral after deductible limits to RRSPs and Rhosps have been reached.

— If your company is making contributions on your behalf to a Deferred Profit Sharing Plan (DPSP) you should consider the implications of this plan along with your RRSP. The company gets a tax deduction for making a contribution to the plan on your behalf, although you don't get such a deduction. On the other hand, if you do make a contribution, income earned by the fund will accumulate tax-free so long as the fund is registered.

— The $1,000 of tax-free investment income (it applies to interest and/or dividend income from Canadian sources) should also be taken into account in your tax planning. Some advisers suggest that until the $1,000 of investment income has been accumulated, a taxpayer should forget an RRSP.

Clearly, every effort should be made to receive the maximum amount of tax-free investment income — and this is truly tax-free, while payments from an RRSP will eventually be taxed. Remember, though, this doesn't shelter the initial capital as does an RRSP.

An RRSP is a fund set aside during your earning years for use after retirement. Contributions (within set limits) reduce current taxable income and, so long as the money remains in registered form, all income and capital gains received by the fund are free of tax. Eventually, the fund is deregistered and transferred free of tax into an annuity. You pay tax on the annuity payments (principal as well as income) as they are received — that is, payments in excess of the $1,000 annual pension exemption if you're 65.

Contributions come from the top slice of current income — income that otherwise would be taxed at the top, or marginal rate. In theory, you defer tax during the high-earning, high-tax years, to repay it when your tax rate should be lower. Assuming you have no other income, the annuity payments will be taxed at the effective rate which is lower than the marginal rate.

There is, of course, no guarantee that your retirement saving will, in fact, be taxed at a lower rate — no matter what the sellers of the plans may tell you. It will depend on inflation (and salary gains) over the years, tax rates and exemptions in the future and your other sources of retirement income.

Still, a growing consideration these days — and one that is turning some toward RRSPs — is the possibility of early retirement. If you are covered by a company pension plan, it probably provides for retirement at age 65 and early retirement will usually produce a much smaller pension. Although the retirement age for full pension benefits in some plans is moving down, it is usually 60 or more. In fact, even if you receive full pension benefits, it may not allow you to live in retirement as comfortably as you would like. Savings from an RRSP might contribute significantly to your enjoyment and security in the future.

Whatever your tax position after retirement, you should be able to build a much bigger pool of savings through an RRSP than if you invest after-tax dollars. The hypothetical example (on page 21) of a man who puts aside $1,000 a year demonstrates the point. After 10 years, his sheltered fund is more than twice as big as that accumulated from after-tax earnings. In 30 years, the sheltered fund is more than three times as big.

Even if the man's annual annuity of $14,700 derived from the RRSP is taxed at a marginal rate of 60% (which implies substantial income from other sources) and the other fund isn't taxed at all, this taxpayer would have more after-tax income from the RRSP fund. Some completely unrealistic assumptions are made

18

in this example — the tax rates, exemptions, interest rates and so forth will remain unchanged for the next 25-30 years, for instance. But whatever assumptions you choose, the fact remains that a fund that is sheltered from tax will grow much faster than one that is not sheltered.

An RRSP likely won't provide all the answers to comfortable retirement living. But it should help — and in the meantime provide a welcome tax deferral.

How retirement income can be split with a spousal RRSP

The spousal RRSP and the $1,000 pension deduction (which includes funds from an RRSP providing the recipient is 65) clearly open up new planning horizons for married couples. The name of the game is to split retirement income between the partners and minimize tax.

In this example, it's assumed that Mr. A is self-employed and can put aside $4,000 of pre-tax savings each year into an RRSP. He and his wife are both 40 years of age and she has no income of her own.

Mr. A compares the future effect of putting all his annual $4,000 contribution into an RRSP for himself or dividing it between his own fund and a spousal plan. In doing the arithmetic, he makes certain rather arbitrary assumptions; his wife will have no other income but Old Age Security when she reaches 65 (today's rates are used); he will have an additional $18,450 of in-

19

come; and the RRSP funds earn 8% a year for the next 25 years. Annuity costs and tax rates for 1976 are used.

Annual increase in after-tax income achieved by splitting income is $3,289. That's a minimum saving of $32,890 over the 10-year certain payment period, and would be even higher if the couple lives longer.

	Contributions divided between own plan and spousal plan		All contributions put in contributor's plan
	Mr. A's fund	Mrs. A's fund	Mr. A's fund
	$	$	$
Amount invested each year	2,000	2,000	4,000
Annual interest earned	8%	8%	8%
Accumulated savings in 25 years..	157,908	157,908	315,816
Annual annuity income*	18,950	17,560	37,900
Other income†	18,450	1,595	18,450
Total	37,400	19,155	56,350
Tax	11,472	3,996	20,147●
After tax income	25,928	15,159	36,203
Annual family income:			
Husband	25,928		36,203
Wife	15,159		1,595
Total	41,087		37,798

*Life annuities guaranteed for 10 years, based on current rates. (With longer life expectancy, rates for women are higher than for men.)
†Mr. A is assumed to be receiving $3,450 combined Old Age Security and Canada Pension Plan (1976 rates) plus $15,000 of other income (including at least $1,000 qualifying for the interest/dividend deduction). Mrs. A. receives $1,595 in Old Age Security benefits (1976 rates).
●Mr. A may claim the age exemption for his wife as well as for himself. Since OAS doesn't qualify for the $1,000 pension exemption, he may not claim such a deduction on behalf of his wife.
Note: 1976 income tax rates are used, assuming a provincial rate of 30.5% of federal tax.
Source: Sidney Dickinson, partner, Creative Planning Insurance Agencies.

How a sheltered fund grows

This example compares the accumulation of savings achieved through annual contributions to an RRSP and through a fund produced from after-tax income.

It assumes the individual can, from the age of 35 on, afford to put aside $1,000 from pre-tax income for retirement. Throughout the period, a 40% marginal tax rate (the rate at which the next dollar of income is taxed) is assumed, and the fund earns interest at an annual rate of 8%.

	RRSP fund $	Non-registered fund $
Savings available for investment annually	1,000	1,000
Tax on capital (assume 40% throughout the period)	nil	400
Net amount invested annually	1,000	600
Interest earned annually	8%	8%
Tax on interest (40%)	nil	3.2%
Net amount of interest credited	8%	4.8%
Accumulated values:		
In 10 years	15,645†	7,480•
In 20 years	49,423†	19,451•
In 30 years (at age 65)	122,346†	38,605•
Annual income started at age 65*	14,700††	4,650°

*Life annuity, 10 years certain and based on current rates.
•No further tax is due on the fund if received as a lump sum.
†Fully taxed if taken as a lump sum.
°Only the interest portion of current payments taxable as received.
††Total amount of annuity payments taxed as received.
Source: Sidney Dickinson, partner, Creative Planning Insurance Agencies.

Your checklist of the RRSP rules

Before making a move, tick these off.

— To be eligible for a deduction from income any year, you may contribute to an RRSP any time during the year and within 60 days after yearend.

A rule to note is that an RRSP contribution made in January or February must be deducted from the previous year's income to the extent that earlier contributions do not reach the deductible limit. If you haven't contributed the maximum allowed for the previous year, and you want to reduce the current year's taxable income, wait until after March 1 to invest in an RRSP.

Technically, the spousal RRSP complicates the timing of contributions. As the law is written, contributions to your own plan (if any) are considered to have been made first — even if, in fact, they aren't.

Suppose you are entitled to contribute $2,500 to an RRSP. Last June you paid $1,000 into a plan for your spouse. In February of this year, you contribute $2,500 to your own plan. Legally, the $2,500 February payment will be considered your contribution for 1975, and the contribution to your spouse's RRSP won't be deductible. However, this timing anomaly wasn't intended and will probably be cleared up in a future amendment. Meanwhile, it's not likely to be enforced in ordinary circumstances.

— If you are self-employed, or not a member of a company registered pension plan, you may put the lesser of 20% of "earned" income (as defined) or $4,000 into an RRSP and claim the contribution as a deduction against income for tax purposes.

If you are entitled or may become entitled to any benefits from a company plan in respect of the year in question, your maximum RRSP is the lesser of 20% of earned income or $2,500. This is reduced by any contribution you make to the company plan for present and/or past service. (Prior to when the federal government tightened up certain contribution provisions, the rules were more generous in certain situations.)

— Despite these limitations, a contribution by your employer to a deferred profit-sharing plan (DPSP) does not limit your contribution to an RRSP. (The employer may deduct contributions to a DPSP on behalf of an employee, but the employee gets no similar deduction.) Nor does a contribution to a Registered Home Ownership Savings Plan (Rhosp) affect your RRSP contribution limits.

— You may contribute to your own plan, you may put it all into a plan for your spouse, or you may divide the contributions between you and your spouse. The spouse may or may not be working at the time of the contribution, and there are no income limitations on the spouse. The only condition is that total deductible contributions may not exceed the amounts outlined above.

— "Earned" income, a vital consideration in calculating the precise amount that may be contributed in any case where the 20% test applies, is normally total income minus certain benefits (such as unemployment insurance), capital gains, investment income and payments from an income averaging annuity. Rental income, however, is included in earned income and thus an RRSP provides some shelter for rental earnings.

"Wages" or "salary" included in earned income is the net figure — after deducting such items as employment insurance contributions, union or professional dues, traveling expenses.

— Lump-sum payments from company pension plans or allowances for long service on retirement, payments from deferred profit-sharing plans and severance payments may be transferred tax-free into your RRSP, providing the transfer is made within 60 days of the end of the year in which the amounts are received. These payments may not be transferred to a spousal plan.

Old Age Security payments and benefits from the Canada and Quebec Pension plans may also be rolled tax-free into an RRSP up to your 71st birthday.

An unfortunate wrinkle in the Income Tax Act results in limiting the amount that may be contributed to a spousal plan when lump-sum payments from pension funds and the like have been transferred to your plan. This is because all such payments, together with regular payments into your own plan, must be deducted in calculating how much you may contribute to the spousal RRSP. The limitation was not intended and the relevant section of the act is another likely candidate for amendment. Meanwhile, Revenue Canada says it will not take those lump-sum payments into consideration when calculating the permissible contributions to a spousal RRSP.

— You may withdraw money accumulated in an RRSP and turn it into annuity at any time up to your 71st birthday when the plan must mature.

The usual procedure is to buy an annuity from a life insurance company at retirement. The fund is transferred tax-free into the annuity and you pay tax each year on income received. You are taxed on the principal as well as the interest. The annuity must be for life and may be guaranteed for any term up to 15 years. It must be payable to the annuitant or jointly to the annuitant and his/her spouse.

(Contributions may continue to be made to a spousal RRSP after the contributing partner has reached 71, providing the recipient is under that age.)

— When money is withdrawn from an RRSP before maturity, the plan is automatically deregistered and you must include the proceeds in income that year. The tax penalty could be very high, and it may not be reduced through the purchase of an income-averaging annuity. One way to get around the problem is to establish more than one RRSP fund. If you need cash, deregister one fund and leave the others intact.

However, this isn't necessary as the law stands. Suppose you have $10,000 in a fund and you need $2,000 for a current emergency. You could instruct the trustee or the insurance company to transfer $8,000 of the money into another registered fund, then deregister the old fund and take the $2,000 you need. You would have to pay tax on the $2,000 but you would have preserved the RRSP status of the remaining $8,000.

Be careful in doing this. The money you want left in the RRSP must be transferred to the new fund (or the money you want removed so transferred) before the cash you want is withdrawn. If you simply take the money, the whole plan is deregistered and you can't re-register any part of it.

— There is, for the moment at least, another method of receiving funds from an RRSP, Revenue Canada's present practice is to tax the principal of a plan that has been deregistered only as the money is received. Income earned by the deregistered fund is taxed the year it is earned.

If, for instance, you deregister a fund worth $10,000, you could arrange to take the income and some of the principal each year for five or 10 years and spread the tax out over that period. This might be a preferable method of receiving the money on retirement — particularly for an individual whose health is not robust or for anyone who objects to having to purchase a life annuity.

Of course, since this flexibility was probably not intended, there is always the danger that the law may be amended to specifically forbid it. But since the department describes this possibility in its booklet *Registered Retirement Savings Plans* (one of the tax information series booklets), it seems unlikely that it could object in the meantime. It would be wise, however, to seek professional advice before doing this.

— If you die before your RRSP matures, the accumulated money (called the refund of premium) is fully taxed. However, if your spouse is the beneficiary, she (or he) may transfer the plan free of immediate tax to an RRSP in her name with all the same provisions and restrictions that applied in the case of your RRSP — providing the spouse had not passed her/his 71st birthday. No other beneficiary may roll the refund of premiums into another RRSP, but any beneficiary may use it to buy an income-averaging annuity.

— You may borrow to make a contribution to your own RRSP, and the cost of the loan is deductible from income for tax purposes. (Interest on a loan to make a contribution to your spouse's RRSP is not deductible, however.) The interest charge is deductible for the calendar year in which you borrow.

Borrowing to make a contribution to an RRSP — or for any other income-producing purpose — does not affect the $1,000 interest-dividend income exemption (which was not the case before the 1975 tax year). You may claim a deduction for the interest cost and for the investment income.

— An RRSP may not be used as collateral for borrowing. If the fund is used this way, the value of the fund is technically included in income that year. If later you pay off the loan, the security is released and the fund has not been affected by your borrowing, you may reduce income that year by the amount added in the previous year.

— If you retire to another country, you should consider the Canadian and foreign tax implications of receiving your annuity payments abroad.

Starting in 1976, Canadian tax law provides for a 25% withholding tax (up from 15%) on payments made to individuals living abroad — unless the rate is reduced by tax treaties Canada has with other countries. Some of the old (and still existing), treaties exempt periodic annuity payments from withholding tax. However, the trend now seems to be to provide for at least some tax (even up to the 25% limit) to be claimed by Canada.

So far, only a few treaties have been signed, but several more are expected soon. Anyone planning to retire abroad should make careful inquiries about the rules as they relate to the country of destination. In any case, lump-sum withdrawals are subject to withholding tax under Canadian law, and this result is generally not altered by the treaties.

If your periodic annuity payments are subject to Canadian withholding tax, you may, if it is to your advantage, file a Canadian tax return. You pay tax on the annuity payments (plus income from other pensions and similar payments, but not investment income) as though you were resident in Canada and make use of all the regular Canadian personal exemptions. If tax calculated on this basis is less than tax withheld at source, the difference is refunded. You may also make arrangements to have withholding tax reduced if you can show that filing a Canadian tax return would result in a smaller tax bite.

Obviously, you must also consider the tax law of the country in which you settle. In some cases, you will be taxed on the interest portion of the annuity payments only — not the return of capital.

Most savers can ignore the investment limitations imposed on RRSP funds. But those who administer their own plans may not — and there are traps for the unwary. Some key rules:

— You may put securities (rather than cash) into an RRSP. Cost to the fund (and, therefore, your contribution for tax purposes) is market value of the securities at the time of transfer.

Effective in 1974 and subsequent years, you are deemed to have disposed of the securities when you transfer them to the RRSP. If they are worth more than adjusted cost, there will be a capital gain — half of which is taxed — the year of the transfer. If there is a loss, however, the Income Tax Act's superficial loss rules apply and the deductibility of the loss will disappear forever. Moral: don't transfer stock losers to an RRSP.

— You can't invest in just anything. In general, qualified investments include cash, deposits, trust company guaranteed investment certificates, bonds issued or guaranteed by the Canadian government (federal, provincial or municipal), debentures of companies whose stock is listed on a Canadian stock exchange, debt securities of credit unions and co-operatives, mortgages on Canadian real estate, listed Canadian stocks, shares and units of Canadian mutual funds and trust company pooled funds, annuities from a Canadian issuer, foreign property up to 10% of total assets.

Thanks to a change in the rules in 1975, Canada Savings Bonds may now be put into an RRSP. So may rights and warrants listed on Canadian stock exchanges and shares listed on prescribed foreign stock exchanges.

One of the common pitfalls to avoid is investing in nonqualified debt securities. Debentures of a company whose shares are not listed on a Canadian stock exchange may not — even though they are considered high-quality securities. This might apply, for instance, to bonds of a subsidiary of a listed company such as a bank or trust company. However, if the security is insured under the Canada Deposit Insurance Corp., the first $20,000 will qualify.

— When a nonqualified investment — such as real estate or an unlisted stock — is acquired, the book value (cost) must be included in income. When such an investment is sold, you may deduct the lesser of the cost (included in income earlier) or proceeds. The second step seems to offset the first, but it is not that simple. The deduction claimed from income reduces your RRSP contribution limit for the year.

— If a qualified investment bought after Aug. 25, 1972, subsequently becomes a nonqualified investment, the trust must pay a tax equal to 1% of the cost for each month that the nonqualified investment is retained. This means that if the plan buys, say, a listed stock that later is delisted, the stock should be sold immediately.

— Be careful not to exceed the foreign-property limit. If more than 10% of the book value of the assets in an RRSP is foreign property, the trust is subject to a tax of 1% of the excess for every month the excess is maintained in the fund. The tax comes out of the fund.

4

What an RRSP can do: a detailed case study

H. L. Mencken once said that the prophesying business is like writing fugues; it is fatal to every one save the man of absolute genius.

While we don't lay claim to absolute genius, we do predict that, in terms of potential taxes that can be saved by Canadian taxpayers in future years, the rules that permit tax-deductible contributions to a spousal RRSP will be of fundamental importance.

Briefly, the regulations permit a taxpayer to use all or a portion of his (or her) personal Registered Retirement Savings Plan eligibility in order to contribute to an RRSP owned by his (or her) spouse.

While the maximum contribution limits have not been increased, most married taxpayers will be able to achieve a tax saving by splitting the receipt of retirement income between husband and wife. This tax advantage is possible because the income flowing from the "spousal RRSP" will be taxable in the hands of the spouse who owns the RRSP, notwithstanding the fact that it was the other spouse who made the annual contributions and took the tax deductions.

We suggest that the availability of the spousal RRSP as a tax planning vehicle constitutes more than sufficient cause for a married taxpayer to reassess his course of action if he is making (or plans to make) voluntary contributions to a pension plan maintained by his employer. He must determine whether or not he can lessen future taxes by making contributions to a spousal RRSP rather than voluntary contributions to a pension plan. If he can, he must then decide whether or not he wishes to contribute to an RRSP owned by his spouse, given the facts of his personal situation. In making the first determination, the facts outlined in this chapter may be of assistance.

While a wife can contribute to a spousal RRSP for her husband provided she has the necessary earned income, in the majority of cases it will be the husband who contributes on behalf of his wife. Most commonly, either the wife has no earned income or less earned income than her husband, or she will have no income or less income than ther husband during their retirement years. For that reason, the subject will be presented here based upon a situation in which it is the husband who makes a choice between a spousal RRSP and voluntary contributions to a pension plan.

For the purpose of illustrating the advantages of a spousal RRSP vs voluntary contributions, we will refer to a hypothetical taxpayer with the following characteristics:

— Age 45, married, wife age 45.

— Earned income of $20,000 per year.

— Member of his employer's pension plan to which he does not make contributions, but to which he may make voluntary contributions each year for past service and/or current service.

— Based upon the employer's contributions to the pension plan made on his behalf, he can anticipate a pension at age 65 of $15,000 per year.

— His spouse at 65 will have no income other than old age security.

— He has available funds in the amount of $2,500 per year to invest, and he wishes to be able to deduct this amount from his taxable income each year.

He will decide, from among the following alternatives (all of which offer tax deductibility of the full $2,500), how to allocate his $2,500 per year:

1. $2.500 annual contribution to his own RRSP.

2. $2,500 annual contribution to an RRSP for his spouse.

3. Some portion of the $2,500 to an RRSP for himself, and the remainder to an RRSP for his spouse.

4. $2,500 voluntary contribution to his employer's pension plan, leaving him no eligibility to contribute to an RRSP for himself or for his spouse.

In making his decision, this individual should give careful consideration to the following:

RRSP flexibility vs voluntary contributions. Voluntary contributions to his employer's pension plan, for either current service or past service, will not provide the flexibility available with an RRSP. Contributions to the pension plan will be locked in until he retires or until his employment is terminated. The pension income derived from his voluntary contributions will begin when he retires, whether he wants the income then or not.

With an RRSP, the individual has the option of deregistering his RRSP and taking a lump sum at any time, or of starting his income from the plan at any time whether he has retired or not. Alternatively, he may delay the receipt and taxation of the income from the plan as late as his age 71. If he contributed to an RRSP for his spouse, she would have the same flexibility with her plan. Ordinarily, the values accumulated from his voluntary contributions will be paid to him as part of his pension from the employer based upon payments to be made for as long as he lives.

While the income from an RRSP can be taken in the form of a life annuity by age 71, prior to the maturity of the plan he also has the option of having his contributions returned to him over a much shorter time if that is his wish. This might be a desirable course of action if a deterioration in his health had shortened his life expectancy, or if the funds accumulated were not substantial enough to produce an adequate monthly income on a life annuity basis. Based upon the present practice of Revenue Canada, this can be accomplished by deregistering and surrendering his RRSP (or in the case of a spousal RRSP, by his wife deregistering and surrendering her plan) and taking the income in the form of a term-certain annuity over a period of, say, five or 10 years, paying tax as the income is received.

The only way in which the man could defer the taxation of his pension income past his retirement date would be to roll it over to an RRSP as it was paid, until he reached the age of 71.

Adjustment of tax withholding. If the individual is attracted to voluntary contributions by the fact that they will be deducted from his pay cheque and therefore will produce an immediate and ongoing reduction in the level of the tax withheld, he should understand that with an RRSP he does not have to wait to benefit until he files his annual tax return and receives his refund. At present, it is the policy of Revenue Canada to permit a taxpayer to request, by a simple procedure, that his employer adjust the level of withholding tax from his pay cheque to reflect his contributions to an RRSP.

Reduction of taxes during retirement. The most significant potential advantage that is available to the individual through the purchase of a spousal RRSP is the minimization of taxes levied on the retirement income upon which he and his wife will be dependent after they reach retirement. This can be achieved by the splitting of retirement income between himself and his wife.

He will have retirement income from his employer's pension plan of $15,000 annually. His wife will have no income of her own except for Old Age Security. If he contributes his annual $2,500 over 20 years as voluntary contributions to his employer's pension plan, the retirement income he receives will fall in on top of his $15,000 pension and be taxed at his own marginal rate. The same situation will exist if he contributes the $2,500 to his own RRSP. However, if he contributes his $2,500 each year to an RRSP for his spouse, the income from the RRSP will be taxable in her hands at a marginal rate substantially less than his own, or possibly (as shown in the example where the spouse has no income other than Old Age Security), no tax will be payable.

Assuming the individual has contributed sufficient funds to produce $1,000 of income at age 65, the table on the following page illustrates that if the $1,000 of annual income were flowing from a spousal RRSP, the taxpayer and his wife would gain $601.60 each year as the result of tax saving. The tax situation is quite different with $1,000 of annual income flowing to the taxpayer either as additional pension income resulting from voluntary contributions or from his own RRSP.

The tax saving achieved in Example 2 of the illustrative table is the result of two factors: first, the $1,000 of income from the spousal RRSP is not taxable in the wife's hands because her personal exemptions exceed her total income; second, the husband saves tax on his remaining income because his pension in-

31

Two examples of how an RRSP works

	Example 1* $1,000 of annual income to husband at 65 from pension or personal RRSP $	Example 2* $1,000 of annual income to wife at 65 from spousal RRSP $
Husband — Pension from employer	15,000	15,000
Pension from employer as result of voluntary contributions, or from personal RRSP	1,000	nil
Canada Pension Plan	1,315	1,315
Old Age Security	1,345	1,345
Total income	18,660	17,660
Wife — Old Age Security	1,345	1,345
Spousal RRSP	nil	1,000
Total income — family	20,004	20,004
Less income tax payable	4,301	3,700
After-tax income	15,703	16,305

Increase in disposable income as a result of tax saved: $602 per year

---

*Tax rates and exemptions used are those for 1974, for Ontario residents. Provincial tax credit is excluded. Scale of benefits for Old Age Security and Canada Pension Plan based on 1974.
Figures are rounded.

come deduction has been increased as the result of borrowing the unused portion of his wife's pension deduction (that is, in this example, the full $1,000, since she has not used any of it). In Example 1, the husband could not borrow any portion of his wife's pension income deduction because, while she did not use it, in order for him to be able to borrow the unused portion, she must be receiving some pension income. Her Old Age Security income is not pension income for the purpose of calculating the pension income deduction.

If the same individual made contributions sufficient to generate income of $4,000 per year at age 65, there would be a tax saving during retirement of $1,338.70 each year if the income was received by his wife from a spousal RRSP, rather than his receiving the $4,000 each year as a result of voluntary contributions to his employer's pension plan or contributions to his own RRSP.

Obviously, the amount of tax saved during retirement by the use of a spousal RRSP rather than voluntary contributions will not be the same in each case; in some instances it will be less than we have illustrated, while in others it will be more. It will depend on a number of factors: for example, the husband's marginal tax rate during retirement; whether or not the wife has substantial income of her own during retirement; and the level of annual income flowing from the spousal RRSP during retirement.

As a general rule, unless the wife's marginal tax rate during retirement will be as high or higher than her husband's, he will obtain some degree of tax saving by making his annual $2,500 contribution to a spousal RRSP instead of as a voluntary contribution to his employer's pension plan or contributions to his own RRSP.

Voluntary contributions for past service. Prior to 1975, voluntary contributions each year for past service would not reduce the taxpayer's eligibility to contribute to an RRSP, as did any contributions he made in respect of current service. However, as a result of changes made in 1975, the taxpayer's eligibility to contribute to an RRSP is reduced not only by the amount of any current-service contributions, but also by the amount he contributes in respect of past service to his employer's registered pension plan. The employee can no longer combine RRSP contributions with past-service contributions to achieve a maximum annual deduction of $5,000.

The employee who has the option of making voluntary contributions to his employer's pension plan is faced with a very clear choice: maximum $2,500 to a personal and/or spousal RRSP or a maximum of $5,000 to his employer's plan ($2,500 current service, $2,500 past service). If an employee can afford to contribute $5,000 annually, he may decide that the extra $2,500 of annual deductible contribution offsets the tax saving during retirement (and the other advantages) of contributing a maximum $2,500 to a spousal RRSP.

If, however, an individual does not have sufficient disposable income to enable him to make voluntary pension plan contributions up to or approaching the maximum $5,000, he would be well advised to weigh very carefully the advantages of contributing to an RRSP, particularly a spousal RRSP.

The taxpayer in our example, who can afford to contribute a maximum of $2,500 annually, would be well advised to refrain from making voluntary contributions for either past service or current service since either type of contribution would reduce his RRSP maximum. If he lowers his annual spousal RRSP contributions in order to obtain disposable income with which to make the voluntary contributions, he has forfeited part of his potential tax saving during retirement, since he is increasing the amount of income taxable in his own hands after his retirement while at the same time decreasing the amount of income taxable at his wife's lower marginal rate.

Employer payment of administrative charges. When considering the tax advantages of a spousal RRSP vs voluntary contributions to a pension plan, it should be noted that some employers pay all or part of the administrative charges in respect of the employee's voluntary contributions. If the employee purchases an RRSP, he will pay his own administrative and sales charges (if any). However, in the ordinary course of events, the tax advantage to be gained from a spousal RRSP in a particular case would have to be unusually small and the charges paid unusually high, in order to make voluntary contributions of a comparable amount an attractive alternative to a spousal RRSP as a method of long-term saving to produce retirement income.

Longer female life expectancy. In most instances, a husband will consider making contributions to an RRSP for his wife with a view of achieving tax relief as he makes the contributions and the splitting of income after retirement. However, if it is a husband's principal objective to utilize a spousal RRSP as a means of creating a predetermined amount of life annuity income for his wife, he should be aware that it will require approximately 6%-7% more in contributions than would be required to create the same amount of life income for a male. This is because of the female's longer life expectancy, as a result of which she would receive payments for a longer time than a male.

Control of the plan. When an individual makes contributions to his own RRSP and/or to an RRSP for his wife, he does so in the knowledge that he and his wife will exercise control over their respective individual plans. He or his wife will be a party to an RRSP contract, the provisions of which cannot be altered without his (or her) consent.

However, an individual who makes voluntary contributions to his employer's pension plan cannot exercise that type of control. Moreover, pension plan provisions vary considerably from one plan to another.

Therefore, before the individual makes voluntary contributions for either current service or past service to his employer's plan, there are a number of important questions to which he should obtain the answers. For example, what is the schedule of priority that has been established in the employer's pension plan to govern payouts in the event the plan is dissolved for any reason, such as insolvency, or because of the bankruptcy of the employer, or because the employer has ceased to carry on business in Canada? Whose claims will be satisfied first?

The plan may provide that the claims of employees to pensions in respect of the employer's contributions will be satisfied first. In such cases, therefore, a return of voluntary contributions to those employees who had made them would be paid from funds remaining in the plan (if any) only after the prior claims had been met. Do the provisions of the employer's pension plan permit the free transfer of the voluntary contributions that have been made by the individual to that pension plan to an RRSP with another carrier? This could be important if, for example, the investment performance of the carrier of the employer's pension plan should prove to be unsatisfactory.

Property of the spouse. An individual, a husband in our example, who is planning to purchase an RRSP for his wife should understand that it will belong to her, notwithstanding the fact that he will make the contributions. In the event of a marital breakdown, for example, the spousal RRSP will be her property.

5

How to avoid the
wrong RRSP for you

Don't let the lust for a tax shelter inhibit your analysis of an RRSP as an investment. This happens often, particularly as the deadline nears.

Many people know they're purchasing a tax-deferral vehicle, but whether the RRSP accords with their financial objectives is open to question. The multiplicity of plans offered by the various financial institutions makes it difficult to compare statistics on the basis of charges, or rates of return. (See the guide to the various plans at the end of this chapter.)

Rates of return and charges are complicated by non-price variables, such as mode of payments, rights of withdrawal, and risk propensity of each plan. For example, Royal Trust's guaranteed fund in early 1976 paid a rate of 9¾% for five years. However, the RRSP holder wasn't permitted to withdraw the funds during that period of time. After the five-year period, there would be a withdrawal charge of 1% to a maximum of $100. At Canada Permanent, the rate of 9½% on its five-year certificate was guaranteed for six months. But it was possible to withdraw at any time, with a fee for withdrawal of 1% to a maximum of $100.

Further complications arise in the area of guarantees and projections. Assuming a $1,000 contribution, a single premium annuity from Great West Life had a guaranteed value of $35,293 vs $30,632 for a similar plan from Westmount Life Insurance Co.

How RRSP incomes vary for different periods

Period	Monthly payment for life*	Minimum payout
	$	$
No minimum guaranteed period	540	
Five-year minimum guarantee	531	31,844
Ten-year minimum guarantee	504	60,480
Fifteen-year minimum guarantee	475	85,500
No minimum guaranteed period, survivor obtains remainder of capital	505	

However, the projected value of Great West Life was $48,587 vs $48,507 at Westmount. Great West Life charged a $40 policy fee plus 6½% of new money, while Westmount Life charged only a $50 fee. For this lower cost at Westmount, the RRSP holder couldn't surrender his plan for five years. From fifth year to 20th year, surrender charges varied to 6% from 10%.

One way to analyze these plans is to classify them according to sponsor — banks, insurance companies, investment dealers —and the securities in the plans, such as stocks, bonds, mortgages. Other features of the RRSP that deserve to receive more attention are the spousal plans and the eligibility of Canada Savings Bonds as investments.

"The switching of plans has also become more popular," says Christopher Snyder, a partner in Executive Compensation Consultants, who has updated his book, *How to Be Sure You Get the Right RRSP*. "People are beginning to realize more and more that the tax-sheltering provisions of an RRSP are given, irrespective of where it's purchased. They're analyzing more thoroughly the performance of their earlier investment decisions.

*For a male, age 65, $50,000 RRSP proceeds, quotations from a major life insurance company.

"If they bought the wrong type of plan, or if the investment experience of their RRSP is marginal, they're more prepared to switch plans today, than when the sole rationale for purchase was tax deferral," he says.

Another situation that poses a problem for the RRSP holder is the purchase of life annuities. Where should it be purchased? What guaranteed period should be arranged? What type of annuity — joint annuities or single-life immediate annuity?

Part of the problem in deciding which company to select is the difficulty of keeping abreast of changing interest rates. Companies use different rates in calculating their annuities. A check in early 1976 showed that six leading companies offered life annuities at different rates. These monthly payments varied from a low of $203.51 to a high of $208.48.

To obtain comparative figures, consult an annuity broker. Since these brokers are paid a commission from life insurance companies, there's usually no charge for this service. As part of the service, they can also arrange guaranteed periods or terms that coincide with your financial situation.

T. W. Brown, president, Annuity Quotations Ltd., says: "As financial affairs become more complex, the shopping around becomes more tedious. People should take advantage of the financial services available to them. In this way they can maximize not only their investment but their well-being."

If you're a do-it-yourself person, remember that life annuities can have two guarantees. In the case of a 15-year-minimum guarantee, you're guaranteed monthly payment for 15 years. If you live beyond that time, the guarantee holds until you die. If you die before 15 years, the money is paid to your survivor until the 15th year. In the case of a cash refund on the early death of the annuitant, there's no minimum guaranteed period, but the annuitant's survivor is entitled to the remainder of the capital. Under the no-refund annuity, the annuitant has only one guarantee — that of receiving payments until death, whether it be one year or 50 years. (See the table opposite.)

Other basic considerations are the deferred-payout commencement date or the possibility of joint annuities (husband and wife).

Following is a guide to the various types of RRSPs.

Type of plan	Issued by	Advantages	Disadvantages
Deposit plans An interest bearing savings account for which a term of years or months need not be specified. The interest rate paid is usually a fraction above prevailing savings account rate.	Banks, some trust companies, credit unions.	1) Rate of return fixed in short term. 2) Excellent liquidity. 3) Principal guaranteed. 4) Can be purchased in small amounts. 5) Flexibility in contributions. 6) Understanding operation of plan is easy.	1) Relatively low yield. 2) Some plans have acquisition and termination charges. 3) No guaranteed annuity or insured death benefits.
Guaranteed investment certificates Certificates issued in set principal amounts and for varying lengths of time.	Trust companies, investment dealers as sub-agents.	1) Guaranteed interest for term chosen. 2) No acquisition costs. 3) Principal guaranteed. 4) Fees minimal. 5) Contributions can be irregular. 6) Understanding operation of plan is easy.	1) Limited liquidity. 2) Penalty for premature withdrawal. 3) No guaranteed annuity or insured death benefits.
Income funds Consists of bonds, mortgages and similar securities such as preferred shares. This pool of securities is divided into units of participation of equal value. It is these units which are purchased at market value with your RRSP contributions.	Banks, trust companies, mutual funds, life insurance companies, investment dealers.	1) Money managed by professionals. 2) Immediate compounding of interest. 3) Diversification. 4) Flexibility in contributions.	1) Variable rate of return. 2) Principal not guaranteed 3) No guaranteed annuity or insured death benefits. 4) Usually fees for setting up, administering and closing out the plan and in some cases front-end load.

Equity-based funds

Consists of common shares of corporations as well as preferred shares, bonds, debentures, in various combinations, depending on fund. Divided into units similar to income fund.

Trust companies, mutual funds, insurance companies, investment dealers.

1) Flexibility in contributions.
2) Potential for long-term growth.
3) Money managed by professionals.

1) No guarantee on principal.
2) No guaranteed annuity or insured death benefits.
3) Fees for setting up, administering and closing out the plan and in some cases front-end load.

Life-insured funds

Savings portion of a life insurance policy is an eligible investment.

Life insurance companies.

1) Insured death benefits.
2) Guaranteed annuity.
3) Policy can be insured against disability within the contract.
4) Forced form of savings.
5) Advice of an insurance agent.
6) In the event of death, if the beneficiary is a wife or child the plan is not subject to claims by creditors in the event of a bankruptcy.
7) Possibility for participating in extra dividends earned by company.

1) Very large front-end load because of early charges and salesmen commissions.
2) Poor liquidity and low rate of return in early years.
3) Limited compounding.
4) Inflexibility in contributions.
5) Guaranteed return on money is poor.

Type of plan	Issued by	Advantages	Disadvantages
Annual-premium annuities Income received from capital on a regular basis. Plan is a series of capital contributions from which the future annuity (the monthly payout) is guaranteed and built-in when purchased. In future, when income is desired, plan gives you option of purchasing annuity at current rate at no extra charge.	Life insurance companies.	1) Plan can be insured against disability within the contract. 2) You may vary contributions up and down. 3) Guaranteed annuity. 4) Forced form of savings. 5) In the event of death, if the beneficiary is a wife or child the plan is not subject to claims by creditors in the event of a bankruptcy. 6) Possibility for participating in the investment experience of the company.	1) Large front-end load because of early charges and salesmen commissions. 2) Poor liquidity in early years. 3) Contributions are contractual. 4) No insured death benefits.
Single-premium annuities Plan is a contribution from which the annuity is guaranteed. Contributions are not contractual.	Life insurance companies.	1) Charges are much lower than the other life insurance plans. 2) Many plans offer fairly high guarantees. 3) Guaranteed annuity. 4) Contributions can be irregular.	1) No insured death benefit. 2) Usually minimum contribution of $1,000. 3) Charges for new contributions. 4) Redemption charges.
Self-administered plans You make investment decisions or hire investment counselor to make them.	Trust companies.	1) Relatively low cost for large portfolios. 2) Success determined by your own resilience and ability. 3) Contributions can be irregular.	1) Somewhat costly on amount less than $10,000. 2) Dividends and interest not automatically invested. 3) No guaranteed annuity or death benefits.

Plan	Available from	Advantages	Disadvantages
			4) Annual administration fee. 5) Must be aware of the many tax rules and investment restrictions.
Canada Savings Bond plans Allows you to invest your CSBs in RRSP.	Vanguard Trust Co., investment dealers.	1) Good liquidity. 2) Interest can be automatically invested in new Canada Savings Bonds. 3) Guaranteed principal and interest for the duration of bond. 4) Minimal acquisition and termination charges. 5) Contributions can be irregular.	1) No guaranteed annuity or death benefits.
Group plans Payments into RRSP can be made either in lump sum or by payroll deduction.	Insurance companies, trust companies.	1) Forced savings if done by payroll deduction. 2) Taxable income is adjusted at time contributions made. 3) In some cases, administration costs are paid by the employer although in such cases the costs are deemed to be taxable benefits to employee. 4) Charges on group plans are often less than most individual plans.	1) Cost of administration for the employer. 2) Change of employment requires individual to leave group plan.

6

Choosing a Rhosp: a lifetime decision

The Registered Home Ownership Savings Plan (usually called a Rhosp) was designed to help the struggling young couple save up to buy a house. And clearly it is widely used for this purpose. As it happens, though, a good many not-so-young and no-so-struggling individuals have also found the Rhosp an ideal savings plan cum tax shelter.

Some more affluent Rhospers are already living comfortably in their spouses' houses. Others, with no thought of house ownership, are using Rhosps to boost retirement savings. It's all because of the very special features of a Rhosp (also sometimes called an R-Hosp or a Hosp, or even, in the case of one plan, a Whosp).

— If money withdrawn from the tax-sheltered Rhosp fund is used to buy an owner-occupied house (and that includes making mortgage payments) or to purchase furnishings for that house or furniture for a spouse's owner-occupied house, the money escapes tax altogether. (See page 48 for a detailed explanation of the Rhosp tax rules.) This legal tax reduction, plus the fact that a principal residence escapes capital-gains tax, makes home ownership particularly attractive.

— If the money isn't used for a house or furnishings, it can be "rolled" tax-free into a Registered Retirement Savings Plan (RRSP), a registered pension plan, or an Income Averaging Annuity (another tax-deferral plan).

44

Obviously, it would be better to escape tax. But deferral has its advantages, too. And since Rhosp contributions don't affect your annual RRSP contribution limits, Rhosping provides a means of building a bigger RRSP fund.

Of course, the Rhosp has had its critics. It frequently is attacked as a "tax gimmick" — and it certainly seems to encourage some shifting of property between spouses for no reason but to reduce tax. Then, many a struggling young home buyer has already blown his chance of ever having another Rhosp (you can have only one in a lifetime) and has used the plan for a one-shot tax reduction. That can hardly have been the idea in the minds of the Rhosp architects.

When the Rhosp first appeared on the scene in 1975, about 210,000 plans were registered — with most of those contributions claimed as deductions from income for the 1974 taxation year. About 20% of the plans were terminated within the year.

A serious drawback is that you may not switch your Rhosp plan from one issuing financial institution to another — as you can with an RRSP. This lock-in is one of the rules designed to ensure that you won't have more than one Rhosp during your lifetime. But it hardly makes for a free, competitive marketplace, and it has been strongly criticized by the Joint Committee on Taxation of the Canadian Bar Association and the Canadian Institute of Chartered Accountants.

Then, too, this supposedly simple plan has turned out to be far from simple. As with so many other tax rules, there has been more than a little confusion — and anguish.

The rule that has caused more confusion than any other is this: you may not claim a deduction from income for any tax year during which you own an interest in residential property in which you or anyone else lives. You may not, in fact, make a Rhosp contribution, then turn around and buy a house in the same taxation year. Unhappily, many individuals still haven't grasped that rule.

Many tax and financial advisers say you shouldn't make a contribution until January or February following the year for which you wish to claim a deduction. In this way, you would avoid problems if you change your mind about buying a house, or in case you inherit one after you have made a contribution. You could, of course, contribute in, say, February 1976, claim the deduction for

1975 tax purposes, and then buy your house in March 1976.

As with an RRSP, Rhosp contributions may be made within 60 days after the end of the year for which the deduction is to be claimed. And that's why the plans are promoted so vigorously in January and February.

Rhosps are sold by trust companies, banks, credit unions, and mutual funds. Unlike RRSPs, they are not available from life insurance companies.

While there are some equity Rhosp funds, most of the plans are invested in bonds, mortgages, fixed-term guaranteed investment certificates, or deposits usually paying rates that are a bit higher than regular nonchequeing savings deposits. There's one plan into which you put your Canada Savings Bonds.

As with RRSPs, fees, rates of interest, minimum investment requirements vary widely. But because you can't switch your plan to another issuer, it's even more important that you shop carefully before you invest in a Rhosp. Some have administration fees ranging from about one-quarter of 1% to three-quarters of 1% a year. There are several with no fees.

When considering one of these plans, establish whether the interest rate quoted is "gross" (before deducting any administration fee) or "net" (after the administration fee). And ask the issuer to give you a record of the rates that have been paid since the plan started. Some companies appeared to offer very favorable rates during the selling season early in 1975, then dropped the rates rather sharply once the deadline passed.

It depends, of course, on your special circumstances whether you can have a Rhosp and if so how you should use it. But here are some planning possibilities:

— If you don't own residential property, consider a Rhosp. And remember, a husband and wife can each have a Rhosp — providing neither owns property. Two Rhosps can help quite a bit toward the down payment on a jointly owned house.

— If you own the family house outright and your spouse doesn't own any residential property — that is, no cottage, farm, ski cabin, or investment residential property — the spouse should consider a Rhosp. It could be used eventually to furnish your house — and "furnishings" cover a broad range of indoor furniture and equipment.

46

— If you and your spouse already own a house jointly, there may be some point in arranging that just one of you owns it outright so the other could set up a Rhosp. (The transfer could be achieved through a sale or a gift — although in some provinces such a transfer might attract gift tax.)

— Then when the spouse with the Rhosp wants to terminate the plan some years hence, he or she could use the Rhosp funds to buy the house from the other or to reduce the mortgage, providing title to the property has changed hands. Then the other spouse could start Rhosping.

Since most first mortgages from major financial institutions carry some restrictions on repayments during the term of the loan, Rhosping to reduce a mortgage may have to be done at anniversary dates.

— A Rhosp can, in some cases, preserve the marriage exemption (or most of it) claimed by the spouse with the larger income. If, say, a wife earns just enough money to wipe out the exemption her husband could have claimed, she might consider contributing to a Rhosp — providing she has no interest in the house or other residential property. She eventually could put the money toward a house or furniture.

— The same principle might be applied in the case of a child who is 18 years of age (minimum age for Rhosping) and who is earning enough money to eliminate the parent's exemption. In this case, the parent might give the money to the child for the contribution. (There will be no complications about eventual attribution of income when money is given to a child of 18 or more.)

Thus the parent gets an exemption for giving his child money. But if you do this, remember you have reduced your child's lifetime contribution limit of $10,000. He might want to claim that deduction himself one day.

— One far-out, and probably short-lived, loophole would seem to permit the temporary tax-sheltering of substantial investment income. It's an unintended side effect of the rules dealing with overcontributions.

Normally, all the money must come out of a Rhosp at one time. However, the tax law provides that where too much has been contributed, the overpayment, plus interest earned on it, may be withdrawn without affecting the rest of the fund. No tax is levied on the amount withdrawn if it is used in the purchase of a house or furnishings.

So an investor might, say, put $100,000 into a Rhosp as an intended overpayment. Later, he would withdraw it, along with the income it had earned; and use the money to buy his house. He wouldn't receive a deduction from taxable income that year, but he would not be taxed on the contribution or the income earned by the fund. Of course, that assumes he could find a trustee who would go along with such a plan. In any case, if that loophole is used much it will certainly be plugged.

Your checklist of the Rhosp rules

The Rhosp has clearly become a household name, but that doesn't mean that everyone knows what it's all about. In fact, it is still surrounded by confusion, and many a saver has come to grief through inadvertently breaking the tax rules. Since Rhosping is a once-in-a-lifetime game, it pays to know the rules before you start. Following is a checklist of a few to keep in mind.

— You may not claim a deduction from income for any tax year during which you owned an interest in residential real property in Canada. That means property in which you or anyone else lives — your home, for instance, or the cottage or residential property you rent to others. And the rule applies whether you own an interest in the property directly, or through a partnership, at any time during the year in question.

You may not own property at the time you establish a Rhosp either. On the other hand, you needn't terminate a Rhosp if, after establishing it and contributing, you acquire residential property in a subsequent year. You may keep the fund registered, allow it to accumulate tax-sheltered income — so long as no contribution is made or deductions claimed for any year of property ownership.

48

Property owned *outside* Canada doesn't affect your eligibility.

— Another important eligibility rule specifies that you may have only one Rhosp during your lifetime. Once you've terminated the plan, you may never establish another one. As the law is written, it also means you may not switch a Rhosp plan from one issuing financial institution to another — as you may with an RRSP. So take special care in choosing your Rhosp plan in the first place.

— The plan must provide for a single payment out of the Rhosp. Except in the case of an excess contribution, where partial withdrawals are permitted, all the money must come out at once.

— To be eligible, you must be at least 18 years of age (there's no upper age limit) and a resident of Canada.

— If you're eligible, you may contribute up to $1,000 a year (with a lifetime maximum of $10,000) and claim the amount contributed as a deduction from income for tax purposes. Like a Registered Retirement Savings Plan (RRSP) contributions and income earned by the fund are sheltered from tax while the plan is registered. Unlike an RRSP, there's no income-related restriction on contributions — just the $1,000 annual and $10,000 lifetime limits.

— Like RRSPs, deductible contributions may be made during the year and up to 60 days after yearend. And since there are penalties for making an ineligible contribution, you would be wise to wait until the following January or February to make a contribution — unless you are certain you won't buy or inherit property during the tax year in question.

If you made a contribution in, say, February 1976, you could have claimed a deduction from 1975 income — providing you didn't own any property at any time in 1975.

You could, though, own property any time in 1976 (unless you were establishing a Rhosp — in which case you couldn't own property at the time of application). Of course if you acquired residential property in 1976, no deduction could be claimed when filing your 1976 tax return.

— Unlike an RRSP, the cost of money borrowed to make a Rhosp contribution is not deductible for income tax purposes.

— Like an RRSP, your Rhosp fund may not be used as collateral for any other borrowing you may do.

— If money from a Rhosp is used to buy an owner-occupied house in Canada, or furnishings for that house or for a spouse's house, the contributions and income earned by the fund may be withdrawn free of tax.

The term "owner-occupied" doesn't mean that you must own the house outright. You could own it jointly with someone else, but you must live in it long enough to establish occupancy. (The occupancy test seems to be a pretty loose one and you probably could qualify after a reasonably short residence.)

Since a husband and wife may each have a Rhosp — providing they are both eligible — they may save together to buy their jointly owned house.

The house or furnishings must be acquired within 60 days after the year in which the money is withdrawn. A "house" may be any housing unit or a share of the capital stock of a co-operative housing corporation.

The money may be put into a down payment or toward the construction of your home. If you are using the funds to finance building, beware of terminating the Rhosp late in the year for the purchase of land, since the house is not likely to be completed within 60 days.

Revenue Canada is interpreting purchase of an owner-occupied house very broadly to include mortgage payments (interest as well as principal). So if you are an owner (or part-owner) and an occupant, Rhosp funds may be used to reduce the mortgage. This enhances the planning possibilities of switching ownership of a house between spouses.

Rhosp money may be used to purchase a broad range of indoor furnishings such as dining-room or living-room suites, curtains, carpeting, and appliances.

While the rules specifically exclude so-called "listed personal property" (defined in the Income Tax Act as prints, etchings, drawings, paintings, sculpture or other similar works of art; jewelry; rare folios; rare manuscripts or rare books, stamps or coins) it appears that tax-free Rhosp money could be used to buy antiques. Outdoor furniture and equipment is specifically excluded.

— If cash is withdrawn from a Rhosp, the money is added to income and taxed the year of withdrawal. And since all the money must come out at once (except in the case of overpayment) and you may not have another Rhosp, it is clear that a Rhosp is no place to invest money you might need for a current emergency.

— On the other hand, if Rhosp funds are not used to buy a house or furnishings, they may be "rolled" into an RRSP or an Income Averaging Annuity, another tax-deferral plan. No tax is paid at the time the money is transferred, and in the case of an RRSP, the transfer doesn't affect the regular annual RRSP contribution limits. Tax is, of course, paid in the normal way on the money as it is received out of the RRSP or income averaging annuity.

This deferral-of-tax opportunity has encouraged many individuals who have no intention of ever buying houses to invest in Rhosps. It is an ideal way for the apartment dweller, who can spare the cash, to boost an RRSP fund from which retirement income will eventually be drawn.

— If you acquire an interest in residential property during the same tax year for which you have already made a contribution to a Rhosp, no deduction may be claimed for that year.

If the money is withdrawn and put into the house or furnishings, it will not be taxed — and from a tax point of view, you will end up as if you hadn't made the Rhosp contribution at all. But you will have terminated the Rhosp and won't be able to have another.

If the money is withdrawn in cash, it will be taxed — and since the deduction is denied, that year's contribution will be subject to double taxation. Even if the money is rolled over into an RRSP or an income-averaging annuity, there will be eventual double taxation.

— Fortunately, there are some remedies — particularly in these early years of Rhosping when there is still widespread confusion about the rules. Revenue Canada has said it will consider the annulment of a Rhosp within one year of the first assessment in which a deduction is claimed. Normally, this would only be considered in cases of hardship. But it seems the tax collector is being particularly lenient where mistakes have been made due to misunderstanding.

Thus annulment might, presumably, be available to an individual who made a contribution for, say, 1974 early in 1975, claimed the deduction when filing a tax return in April, and then mistakenly made a second but ineligible contribution for 1975. If the plan is annulled, the individual could at some other time have a Rhosp. But the 1974 tax return would have to be recalculated to eliminate the deduction claimed.

Application for annulment must be made through the trustee — who may or may not be the issuer.

Since annulment by Revenue Canada would be necessary only if the plan had been formally registered — which could be some time after the plan is sold — it may be possible for the trustee to return the money prior to registration.

— For anyone who makes an ineligible contribution in a later year, the solution obviously can't be either annulment (if it's after the time limit noted above) or a pre-registration withdrawal.

Suppose you had contributed $1,000 for four years. In the fifth year, you contribute $1,000 in May and later inherit a house into which you move in December. You could, of course, put the $5,000 plus interest into the house, mortgage, or furnishings. You wouldn't be able to claim a deduction for the $1,000 contributed that year, but you wouldn't be taxed on any of the fund. However, you'd never be able to have another Rhosp.

An alternative would be to treat the $1,000 ineligible contribution together with any interest it had earned, as an overpayment. If withdrawn within 120 days after yearend (that is, by the end of April the following year) and put into a house, mortgage, or furnishings, it would not be taxed and it would not affect the Rhosp status of the remaining $4,000. The fund could remain registered, earning tax-free income even while the house is owned and, if the house is later sold, you could start contributing again.

There is a penalty in using the overpayment technique to correct one year's mistake. An overpayment is counted as a contribution in arriving at the lifetime limit of $10,000, even though the ineligible contribution is not deductible.

— When the owner of a Rhosp dies, all the money is deemed to have been distributed to him and the amount fully taxed the year of death — *unless* the individual's will authorizes the executors to use the money to reduce a mortgage or buy furnishings for the home that was owner-occupied by the deceased at the date of his death, or to buy furnishings for the owner-occupied home of the deceased's spouse.

52

Obviously authorization of a mortgage payment or purchase of furniture for your own house would only be relevant if you had established a Rhosp before acquiring property, then kept the fund registered after acquiring a house and ceasing to contribute.

The law also allows a spouse to receive the Rhosp on a temporary basis. He or she would have 15 months to buy a house or furnishings, put it into an RRSP, or buy an income-averaging annuity. Since this transfer would be possible even if the spouse had a Rhosp, it is the one circumstance in which an individual might, for a short time, have an interest in two Rhosps.

However, while the tax rules provide for such a designation through the plan, provincial law prevents the money from going directly from the Rhosp to the spouse. Similar difficulties with RRSPs have been overcome in some provinces, but nowhere has the Rhosp problem been dealt with yet.

It means that if you plan to make your spouse the beneficiary in the event of your death, be sure to make specific provision for this in your will as well as through the plan.

7

Moving your money
ahead of the tax man

If you've won a cash prize or received a lump sum, or if you're a hockey star, a successful novelist or an opera singer, it may well be to your advantage to look at an Income Averaging Annuity Contract, or IAAC (pronounced "yak" or "eye-ack").

You should certainly study the rules and advantages if you've realized substantial capital gains, face recaptured depreciation, wound up a business or, indeed, if you have received significant income from any of the sources outlined in the list at the end of this chapter.

Designed to let an individual taxpayer spread unusually large receipts of *specified* types of income over the current and future years, an IAAC provides a deferral of most of the tax on this special income while restricting the use of the income to a fixed yield. You put most of the qualifying income into a special annuity, then pay tax on the return of capital and interest as payments are received in the future.

Like the RRSP and Rhosp, an IAAC may be purchased any time during the tax year in question or in the first 60 days after yearend.

The IAAC is a creature of the "new" (post 1972) tax system. Use of the IAAC is usually called "forward averaging" and is one of two new methods of softening the tax blow when an unusual amount of income is received in one year. The other method, called general averaging, is applied automatically by Revenue Canada when income in any year exceeds the previous years' levels by specified percentages.

Unlike forward averaging, general averaging is available for all types of income received by Canadian residents. But for higher-income individuals, general averaging won't usually, by itself, be as attractive as forward averaging.

Then, the IAAC has some special twists — some say anomalies — that may prove particularly rewarding for you. The IAAC should, of course, be examined along with RRSPs and Rhosps and be taken into account in your total tax and financial planning.

Following are some of the IAAC's special features and some planning points to keep in mind:

— An IAAC lets you defer tax, and deferral is like an interest-free loan from the government — money on which you can earn income. It may also result in a reduction in tax — if, for instance, inclusion of all the special income in any one year would push you into a higher tax bracket or if, during the next few years, your income declines materially.

All things being equal, indexing of the tax system (at present personal exemptions and tax bracket boundaries are indexed) will tend to reduce tax on future annuity payments if your total income remains constant. (Another chapter looks at tax indexing.) However, the future tax bite will obviously be influenced by tax rates — and who dares predict how these will move?

— As with an RRSP, you may borrow to buy an IAAC, invest the proceeds in income-producing assets, then claim the borrowing costs as a deduction from taxable income the year the interest expense is incurred. Unlike an RRSP, an IAAC may be used as collateral for a loan. All this gives you considerable flexibility and enables you to avoid impairing your investment capital.

It depends, of course, on interest charges at the time of borrowing whether this is an attractive proposition. In any case, if you're likely to use an IAAC as collateral, choose the annuity carefully or buy more than one. You may have trouble borrowing against some annuities, such as non-commutable life contracts.

— Use of an IAAC to forward-average capital gains, together with the tax law's capital-loss carry-back and carry-forward provisions, enables you to have your cake and eat it. You may carry losses back or forward in the normal way and reduce taxable gains just as though you hadn't bought an IAAC. The result is to reduce ordinary income.

Let's suppose you had $10,000 of excess 1974 deductible losses available for carrying forward to 1975. (You must offset all gains and $1,000 of ordinary income in the current and carry-back years before remaining losses may be carried forward.)

In 1975 you had $20,000 of net capital gains and you decided to forward-average. You must include in income an amount equal to one annual payment from the IAAC and, assuming this is $2,000, you would put $18,000 into an IAAC. Ordinary income in 1975 was $50,000.

Now assume that in 1976 you had $10,000 of excess losses (after claiming the maximum for that year) available to be carried back to 1975.

When filing your 1975 income-tax return, you would show $42,000 of taxable income ($50,000 plus $2,000, minus the $10,000 of loss carry-forward from 1974).

When calculating your 1976 tax, you could carry the $10,000 of excess losses back, recalculate 1975 tax, reduce taxable income for that year to $32,000 and claim a refund.

— If your special income is money taken out of a registered pension plan or deferred profit-sharing plan, pause to consider the best strategy for you. Some of that money brought into income may be averaged according to the old (pre-1972) tax rules. To the extent you had a credit on Jan. 1, 1972, you can use the old rules. Basically the old rule involved spreading the amount that must be included in income over previous years and the current year. Whether you're better off with this method, or with forward-averaging, depends on many factors. As a general rule, if income — and therefore the marginal tax rate — has been high during the past few years, the old rules may not be an advantage. If, on the other hand, you had a few low income years, or a loss in a sole proprietorship, the old rules might suit you well. In this case the average tax rate of the previous three years would be applied to the appropriate amount of income.

— Certain lump-sum payments, such as those from pension funds on retirement, which qualify for forward averaging, might better be "rolled" into an RRSP — providing you haven't reached

71 years of age. If income from an annuity bought with RRSP money is received after the age of 65, it qualifies for the pension exemption of up to $1,000 a year. Income from an IAAC doesn't qualify for this exemption.

— You should also consider the exemption for up to $1,000 of interest and/or dividend income. Interest earned on an IAAC doesn't qualify for this exemption, and if you aren't already receiving enough investment income to take full advantage of $1,000 deduction, pause before you put all your special income into an IAAC.

Remember too, forward-averaging gives you a deferral of tax, but it restricts you to a fixed yield. If you invest after-tax proceeds, you have the possibility of making a capital gain. You can also take advantage of the tax credit that Canadian dividends provide and the special tax treatment of capital gains.

It may, in short, be to your advantage to pay tax on some of your special income this year and forward-average the rest. Your wisest strategy will depend on a number of factors such as the amount of special income, tax rates, and your other sources of investment income.

— IAAC's are sold by life insurance companies and most large trust companies. Loyalty to a company you regularly do business with shouldn't be a consideration when buying an IAAC. It pays to shop around, as the survey at the end of this chapter shows.

Plans are normally sold on the basis of an individual quotation. You submit an averaging plan (naming the amount of qualifying income and the number of years over which you want to average) to a variety of issuers, and choose the best offer. Rates may vary significantly from company to company and may change daily. Normally a rate is maintained for an individual customer for a few days after it's quoted.

A number of financial consulting firms offer quotation services and will do the leg work for you. This service shouldn't mean an additional cost — unless there's a considerable amount of extra planning advice involved — because the firm is normally reimbursed by the IAAC issuer through a finder's fee.

Study the implications of the various terms. You can have a life annuity or one with a specified term (subject to certain limitations). Your choice will depend on your age, health, present and prospective financial and tax position as well as those of your heirs.

— Forward-averaging is available through purchase of an IAAC by a Canadian resident individual, but an estate, trust, partnership or corporation won't qualify.

— Any of the types of income in the list at the end of the chapter may be used to buy one or more IAACs from any Canadian organization licensed to issue such contracts.

— The annuity may be for life (only life companies can sell these) with or without a guaranteed term. Or it may be for a specified term without a life contingency. Maximum guaranteed term, whether it's a life annuity or not, is the lesser of 15 years or 85 years minus the age of the individual at the time his annuity payments begin. This means that anyone over 70 when payments start won't be able to arrange a 15-year term.

— As noted above, an IAAC may be bought any time during the taxation year in which the qualifying income is received and up to and including the 60th day after yearend. Most years, the deadline is March 1.

— Annuity payments must start within 10 months after purchase of the IAAC. Thus, if you'd bought an IAAC on March 1, 1976, you could have deferred receipt of the first payment to Jan. 1, 1977, and so avoided any tax on the special income during 1976. When considering an IAAC, assess the advantages of the March 1 purchase well in advance and at least start window-shopping early. Annuity rates have a habit of declining as March 1 approaches.

— Once payments start, they may be received at any interval if at least one comes in each year of the contract. The return on monthly payments will usually be better than on annual ones.

— You must pay for the IAAC in a single premium, deductible from taxable income the year you receive the qualifying income. The maximum you may deduct is the total of income qualified for forward-averaging less an amount equal to an annual payment under the annuity contract.

In other words, you must include in current income at least as much as one of the annual payments you'll receive in future years. You pay tax on the income (principal as well as interest) as it is received.

58

Let's suppose you receive $50,000 of special income in Year A†
— from one or more qualifying sources. Assume also, that your
ordinary income is $60,000 and your personal exemptions total
$3,622 (married-couple, plus the $100 standard charity-medical
deduction).

You decide to forward-average all of the $50,000 that you can.
For illustrative purposes, assume that you buy a 15-year-certain
annuity, that the cost of the premium is $44,222 and annual in-
come is $5,778. You'd include the $5,778 in Year A's taxable income (or, put another way, you would deduct the $44,222 pre-
mium). And here's how Year A's tax would compare with and
without forward averaging:

	With	Without
	forward averaging	
	$	$
Ordinary income	60,000	60,000
Taxable portion of		
special income	5,778	50,000
Total income................................	65,778	110,000
Less: personal		
exemptions.............................	3,622	3,622
Taxable income	62,156	106,378
Tax*...	28,181	52,997**

With forward-averaging, tax on the additional $5,778 of in-
come would be $3,241 or about 56%. Gross income received over
16 years (Year A and the next 15 years) would be $92,448 and, as-
suming the same tax rate over the next 15 years, total after-tax income would be $40,592.

If instead of applying forward-averaging, you include the
$50,000 in Year A's income, tax on this special income would be
$28,057 or 56%, after applying general averaging. Assuming the
after-tax income of $21,943 is invested at 10% (approximate yield

†Year A is 1975 for the purposes of these specific calculations.
*Assuming provincial rate of 30.5% of federal tax.
**General averaging has been applied assuming income in the years 1972-74 was $55,000.
$50,000 and $45,000

59

for the IAAC in the above example) annual income will be $2,194 for a total of $32,910 in 15 years. Then if the interest is taxed at 56%, your total after-tax interest income plus the $21,943 principal would be $36,423 — or $4,169 less than with forward-averaging.

However, the picture might be different if some or all of the $1,000 of investment income exemption could be applied to the interest, or if dividend income were received or capital gains realized.

— As already noted, payment for an IAAC must be in the form of a single premium. However where qualifying income is subject to withholding tax at source — in the case of a salaried athlete, for instance — a special arrangement might be made to direct income toward the IAAC as it is earned.

This strategy involves establishment of a trust into which the employer puts, say, one half the monthly salary. The employer then withholds tax on the other half and distributes the remainder to the individual. This must be approved by Revenue Canada, which will provide a waiver for tax on the portion of income directed to the trust. At the end of the year, the individual decides how much is to be put into an IAAC. But any interest earned by the trust must be reported as income by the employee that year, and any payment to the trust that doesn't flow into the IAAC must be returned to the employer who'll deduct tax and distribute the rest.

— You may not commute or cancel the annuity or change its terms before maturity and still retain the tax deferral. If you do either, the full current value of the contract is added to the taxable income that year. This suggests you might be wise to have more than one IAAC to provide for selective cancelation.

Some contracts don't provide for commutability, and this should be checked out in advance. A life annuity, for instance, is rarely commutable. Note too, that few issuers will actually include the commutability feature in the terms of the contract — presumably to preserve the tax status of the contract. But most will give you the terms verbally and in a letter.

Generally the issuer discounts the contract if it is canceled prior to maturity. A typical arrangement now is to discount the contract to give the issuer 1% more than the company's current investment return. Sometimes there is an additional penalty.

— Until recently, the IAAC appeared to provide an ideal way of reducing tax if you left Canada and took up residence abroad. But that advantage seems to be diminishing.

Starting in 1976, Canadian tax law provides for a 25% withholding tax (up from 15%) on payments made to individuals living abroad — unless the rate is reduced by the various tax treaties Canada has with other countries. These treaties are in the process of renegotiation. Some of the old (and still existing) treaties exempt certain periodic annuity payments from withholding tax. However, the trend now seems to be to provide for at least some tax (even up to the 25% limit) to be claimed by Canada. In any case, lump-sum withdrawals are subject to withholding tax under Canadian law, and this result generally isn't altered even by the old treaties.

So far, only a few of the new treaties have been signed, but several more are expected. If you're planning to leave Canada and have an IAAC, or you're thinking of establishing one, you should keep abreast of the treaty situation. You should also study the tax law of the country to which you move. In some cases, you'll only be taxed on the interest portion of annuity payments — not the return of capital. This advantage must be considered in the context of likely Canadian tax.

— If you die before maturity of an IAAC with a guaranteed term, subsequent payments may be made to a specified beneficiary without disqualifying the contract for income-tax purposes. The beneficiary would add subsequent payments to his income as he receives them.

The types of special income that qualify for forward-averaging

Net capital gains (taxable gains minus allowable losses).

A single payment received from a pension plan.

A single payment on retirement in recognition of long service.

A single payment received from an employee's profit-sharing plan, or from a deferred profit-sharing plan, to the extent that either is required to be included in income in the year of receipt.

Employee stock-option benefit.

Refund of premium from a Registered Retirement Savings Plan on death of the annuitant. The annuitant himself may not roll an RRSP into an IAAC, but a beneficiary may do so.

Payment from a Registered Home Ownership Savings Plan. In this case, the original Rhosp investor may roll the fund into an IAAC.

Payment for loss of office to the extent it is required to be included in income the year of receipt.

Income from activities as an athlete. This is restricted to income received as a direct result of some physical exercise as a competitor or contestant, a Revenue Canada bulletin says. Not included: fees for endorsements, royalties, or teaching income.

Income from activities as a musician or public entertainer — such as an actor, dancer or singer but not usually a radio or TV commentator or announcer, an agent or impresario.

Income from production of a literary, dramatic, musical, or artistic work.

A prize for achievement in the taxpayer's field of endeavor.

Proceeds of the sale of goodwill or other eligible capital property.

Recaptured depreciation.

Income arising from the sale of inventory and accounts receivable on termination of a business.

Death benefits, such as those paid by an employer.

Income from the disposition of certain resource properties.

Proceeds of disposal of an income interest in a trust.

How IAAC rates can vary

Comparative shopping pays off when it comes to buying an IAAC. As this survey shows, rates can vary sharply from institution to institution. In fact, based on rates shown below, you could end up with nearly $4,000 more total income over the life of a five-year contract — depending on which annuity you bought. The difference could be more than $6,000 depending on your choice of a 15-year term.

Then, just to add to the excitement of buying an IAAC, rates can fluctuate almost daily at any one institution.

This representative list of rates was prepared early in 1976 by Sidney Dickinson, founder of Annuity Consulting Services and a partner in Creative Planning Insurance Agencies Ltd., Toronto. Calculations assume $50,000 of qualifying income and that the initial payment has been deferred for 10 months — the maximum deferral permitted under the income-tax rules.

Monthly payments for contracts with terms of

	5 years	10 years	15 years
	$	$	$
Canada Life	856	570	477
Canada Trust	879	591	502
City Savings & Trust	888	597	496
Confederation Life	854	574	477
Crown Life	823	568	481
Industrial Life	861	576	477
Manufacturers Life	841	563	467
Monarch Life	860	579	482
Mutual Life	857	578	483
Royal Trust	871	588	491
Sun Life	845	576	484

8

How a private plane
can pay its own way

Herb Cunningham is something of an anomaly.

Flying these days is not cheap. You can count on at least $30 an hour rental charges for the slowest pair of wings. If you buy your own, you're looking at anything from $15,000 to infinity — plus maintenance and operating costs.

Yet Herb Cunningham flies regularly. He owns, wholly or in partnership, eight aircraft — the figure has been as high as 12 — and he does it on the salary of a high-school math teacher.

How does he do it? By leasing out his planes. Without the leasing arrangements he's made, Cunningham readily concedes he couldn't afford to own and fly aircraft. Neither could many others across Canada.

Here, simplified, is how it works:

You lease your aircraft to a flying school, club or commercial operator, usually with the provision that you may rent it back for your own use at the going hourly rate. The lessee pays you either a fixed monthly fee or a percentage of what he gets when he rents the aircraft out to other pilots. However the payments come, hopefully they cover your loan payments (assuming you financed the purchase) with a little cushion besides.

The most popular aircraft-leasing arrangement in Canada is the "dry lease." This means the lessee administers the aircraft, looks after maintenance, insurance, fuel and oil and pays the owner a fixed sum for every hour the aircraft is rented out.

Sounds a little too neat, having someone else pay for your plane for you? Well, there are catches. For one thing, the situation described above is greatly simplified; leases can be extremely complex and should be tailored to individual situations.

Perhaps the best caveat on the first step comes from accountant Dave Sutton of Thunder Bay, himself a part-owner of a leased aircraft: "Make sure you get good tax and legal advice before you sign."

Utilization of the aircraft by the lessee is the linchpin that can make or break the deal, Sutton emphasizes. "If the lessee doesn't generate enough business to cover your costs, you're still on the hook for the payments on the plane."

Bob Sandoz, a Halifax film producer who's on his second one-year lease with the Halifax Flying Club for his Comanche, figures he lost about $4,000 on the operation of the plane in his first lease. However, the plane was invaluable to him for his business and, with adjustments to the original lease, he's satisfied the arrangement can work for both himself and the club.

Sandoz offers the following tips to would-be aircraft lessors:

— Include a clause specifying how much experience pilots must have before renting from the lessee.

— Insist all repairs over $50 required away from base be authorized by phone by the club engineer.

— Try to get a guaranteed fee that's enough to cover your monthly payments and expenses. "But," says Sandoz, "don't destroy a good relationship by pushing for it. You have to realize the club could get caught if prolonged bad weather interferes with flying. Most clubs are nonprofit."

— Agree on some arrangement for payment in the event the aircraft is grounded for repairs. This might be included in the minimum-rate agreement, says Sandoz.

— Be fair with the lessee. Avoid pre-empting other potential renters to fly the aircraft yourself.

In fact, he adds, put a clause in the lease so you can't: "It's the best way to keep good relations with the lessee who, after all, is looking after your investment."

Commercial operators are also lessees of large fleets of light aircraft. For instance, Staron Flight in Vancouver, which leases 16 and owns three planes, offers flight training, rentals to accredited pilots — and aircraft sales and service.

Steve Saklas of Staron admits an offer to lease back an airplane from a potential buyer is an attractive sales feature. But he insists that "if the plane isn't needed on the line, we won't lease it. Otherwise, it won't be used enough and both the owner and we lose money."

Unfortunately, Staron's scruples aren't universal among dealers, according to a spokesman from a Vancouver distributor of light aircraft parts: "You can bet the planes the dealer owns are rented before any leased ones go up," he claims. "If the dealer doesn't have the volume of rental business, lessors lose."

Pitfalls notwithstanding, the benefits in leasing out an aircraft are attractive enough to interest even non-pilots into buying aircraft.

Why would a non-flyer want to own a plane? Consider some of the tax advantages:

For an owner who leases an airplane to an operator, the plane becomes a piece of business equipment — and the owner can claim capital cost allowance (depreciation) of up to 40% of its value, the amount calculated each year on the declining balance. So, on a $40,000 aircraft, the owner may reduce his *total* taxable income by $16,000 (40% of $40,000) in the first year. The next year, he may claim $9,600 (40% of $24,000), and so on until the plane is depreciated on the owner's books to almost nothing.

In theory, this is really a deferral of tax, because eventually the income from leasing will exceed the amount of capital cost allowance that may be claimed. One way of postponing tax longer is to buy another plane at this point, lease it and go through the exercise again.

Then, as accountant Sutton points out, the day of reckoning probably comes when the plane is sold. If, as is usually the case, the plane sells for more than its undepreciated capital cost (its value on the owner's books after several years of claiming capital cost allowance), the owner is faced with "recapture." This means he must add into his taxable income the amount of depreciation he has claimed but not suffered. That is, he must pay income tax on the difference between the original purchase price and the depreciated value of the aircraft on his books. In fact, he's now paying tax that he has been deferring all along. And it all must be included in income for the year of the sale.

If, for instance, the $40,000 aircraft has been depreciated to $8,640 (after three years of claiming 40%) and is sold for $45,000, the owner will have to add $31,360 ($40,000 minus $8,640) to his taxable income the year of sale. He'll also have to pay tax on $2,500, or half the capital gain.

Could he escape recapture and capital gains tax by selling for an unreasonably low amount to a relative or business associate? No: in the case of a non-arm's length transaction, the aircraft would be deemed, for tax purposes, to have been sold at fair market value. This "fair market value" is then substituted for the book value of the plane in Revenue Canada's calculations. In other words, if you sell for $1, your income in that year will be deemed to have been augmented by $39,999.

What if claiming the full 40% adds up to more than the owner's entire taxable income? In that case, he will claim less than 40% — there's nothing to say he has to claim the maximum.

Or he might establish a partnership to share the cost and expense deduction with others. This was the solution for Dr. Rod Landymore of Halifax who joined with a medical colleague to buy a $100,000 Twin Seneca, now leased to the Halifax Flying Club.

"The opportunity for such an aircraft was there and we wanted the advantage of claiming capital cost allowance," Landymore says. "But we also made the investment so we can fly at cost." The club, he points out, couldn't have afforded such an aircraft.

In addition to sharing the initial expense of purchase, taking a partner or partners will keep your capital cost allowance deferral a little more realistic in terms of your income — and in the eyes of Revenue Canada officials who love to sniff around schemes such as these. The total amount of capital cost allowance to be claimed is determined at the partnership level and is then usually divided among the partners on the basis of each one's share of the original investment.

Still another tax break for lessors comes at the time of purchase, points out John Fitzgibbon who leases his $35,000-plus Mooney Ranger to the Brampton Flying Club. Planes that are leased are commercially registered and are exempted from federal excise tax (10%), federal sales tax (12%) and possibly from provincial sales tax, depending on your province.

"It means I can buy a plane to lease to the flying club," says Herb Cunningham, "for the same price I'd pay in the U.S." Which, in his case, as an Ontario resident subject normally to 5% sales tax, means a price at least 27% lower than that paid by a private owner-operator.

Herb Cunningham, in addition to being a pilot-owner-lessor, is president of the Experimental Aircraft Association of Canada. Ostensibly an organization formed to encourage homebuilders of aircraft, the chapter of the EAA to which Cunningham belongs has also evolved into a flying club almost totally committed to leasing.

The club operates some 15 aircraft, 12 of which it leases from members. Each of the 150 club members pays an initiation fee of $50, purchases a share in the club for $250 and pays monthly dues. This entitles him to use any of the club aircraft on which he has had sufficient recent flying experience just as if they were his own.

Since members must be approved by the board of directors and must have a pilot's licence, owners' planes are protected from inexperienced people.

A non-profit operation, the club offers members cheaper rates per hour than most commercial operators, a wide variety of well-equipped aircraft and a fee structure based on actual hours the plane is in the air rather than the hours it is away from base.

"It's an advantage many members use," says Doug Eberts, who leases a float plane to the club. "The logs of some of the high-performance aircraft we operate show destinations like Texas, Florida and Mexico."

Recent economic conditions have helped bring about a turnover of club equipment. The U.S. recession and heavy new-plane taxes in Canada have made used aircraft more valuable, in some cases, than when they were new. Owners are freqently anxious to sell in such a marketplace.

The variety of club aircraft is controlled since the club membership, through its election of the board of directors, determines what additions would be most used by members.

Ultimately, says Cunningham, the real winner from the owning-and-leasing game isn't so much the investor whose stable of aircraft keeps growing. "The smart owner leases the plane out for a few years and claims the capital cost allowance until the plane starts earning more revenue than he'd like to have to pay tax on. At that point he can quit the lease but he has some equity in the aircraft. If he were to sell, he'd have to pay recapture tax and possibly tax on capital gain. If he keeps leasing he pays income tax on rental revenue."

A financial Gordian knot? "Not quite," observes Cunningham, perhaps a little wistfully, as the part owner of eight aircraft. "If the guy is content just to maintain the aircraft for his own use, he's had a good part, if not all of it, paid for by somebody else.

"If you really love flying, it isn't that expensive once you own your own aircraft outright."

How a leasing deal works

Interested in owning a Cessna 172 for five years and coming out of it more than $4,000 to the good? Accountant (and aircraft owner) Dave Sutton, of Stille, Sutton & Co., Thunder Bay, shows in the accompanying table how it can be done through leasing.

This example assumes two pilots finance the purchase of the new $25,000 plane at 12% amortized over five years. They lease it to an operator and realize $9 every hour the lessee rents it out. Assuming the plane is rented 500 hours a year, which would still leave the owners time to fly it, the profit and loss statement might look like the five-year table on the opposite page.

Though the example is not a sound business venture, concludes Sutton, the owners' net cash outlay in five years would be only $8,418 after tax consideration. And since the plane would have low engine time, resale value might more than make up for the deficiency.

Should the partners wish to sell after five years — for, say, $20,000 — their situation might be as follows:

Proceeds of sale............................	$20,000	$20,000
Less: current book value...............	1,944	
Taxable income	18,056 at 40%	7,222
Net proceeds of sale......................		12,778
Overall result:		
Net proceeds of sale......................		12,778
Plus: tax saving over		
five years...............................		4,732
Less: cash flow deficiency.............		17,510
over five years.........................		13,150
Net cash income...........................		4,360

To turn leasing into a pure business deal, Sutton suggests the plane would have to be rented out more — say, 1,000 hours a year. The doubled rental revenue ($9,000) would produce a good cash flow (albeit doubling the engine overhaul reserve fund), a cash surplus over five years of $6,850, a loss for tax purposes of $3,880 in the first year, and a fully paid-for aircraft at the end of five years. If the plane were then sold for $20,000, net cash income would be $8,315 after taxes.

The five-year record of a paying aircraft-leasing proposition

	Year 1	Year 2	Year 3	Year 4	Year 5	Total
Rental revenue	4,500	4,500	4,500	4,500	4,500	22,500
Expenses:						
Interest	1,630	1,630	1,630	1,630	1,630	8,150
Engine overhaul reserve	625	625	625	625	625	3,125
Capital cost allowance - 40% ...	10,000	6,000	3,600	2,160	1,296	23,056
	12,255	8,255	5,855	4,415	3,551	34,331
Profit (loss) for tax purposes	(7,755)	(3,755)	(1,355)	85	949	(11,831)
Cash flow						
Revenue	4,500	4,500	4,500	4,500	4,500	22,500
Disbursements:						
Loan payments	6,630	6,630	6,630	6,630	6,630	33,150
Engine overhaul ..	—	—	—	—	2,500	2,500
	6,630	6,630	6,630	6,630	9,130	35,650
Cash (deficiency)	(2,130)	(2,130)	(2,130)	(2,130)	(4,630)	(13,150)
Tax cost savings (assuming 40% tax bracket)	3,102	1,502	542	(34)	(380)	4,732

9

The right way to invest in gemstones

Betty Boop used to sing in her panting, pediatric way, "Daddy, I want a diamond ring . . ."

Whether she got the ring is of little consequence. But if she did manage to wheedle a diamond — or an emerald, or even a topaz or two — of decent quality out of daddy, then almost certainly Ms. Boop's rock will not only have weathered the ravages of inflation but have turned her a tidy profit.

Investing in gemstones can be an interesting and rewarding diversification for investors with an already sound portfolio. Just how interesting is a point well made by international gemmological expert Paul E. Desautels in his book *Gem Kingdom*: "Gems combine high value with small size. They are easy to transport, easy to conceal and easy to convert into money. In times of stress when the value of money was weakened, gems have often been the means of saving the value of an estate. Real estate holdings may not survive a revolution, but . . . gems may outlast any political system. Gems are also useful as an instrument of investment. With expanding populations and increasing prosperity in many countries of the world, the number of potential customers for gems — as for paintings and other works of art — is increasing far more rapidly than the available supply. This has had the effect of steadily driving up prices."

If that leaves you wondering why on earth you've been salting away your surplus dollars in stocks and bonds — take heart. Traditional forms of investment — securities, life insurance, real estate — should still be the mainstay of your portfolio. Precious stones, say experts in the trade, should be a facet of it. And not without good reason.

"Unlike stocks and bonds," cautions a diamond trader, "diamonds cannot be turned into cash immediately simply by calling your broker. They can always be sold, but it may take time and effort to find a buyer — just as it does with objects of art and paintings."

Generally, gemstones have appreciated steadily in value over the years. This, along with their portability and their convertibility to cash throughout the world, has made them a favored form of investment for years in Europe. Whereas North American interest in their investment potential is fairly recent.

And, as many are now discovering, there are two routes into the gemstone market: you can deal through a retail jeweler or, by getting deeply involved at the trade level, you can in effect become a gemstone dealer in a small way.

For starters, let's say you opt for the retail route. A leading Toronto jeweler offers this advice: "For investment purposes, there is no point in looking at regular medium-priced jewelry. The jeweler has to take his full markup — or he'll lose money — and that cuts down the investment potential of the piece. Moreover, the stones used in medium-priced jewelry are plentiful.

"Go to a jeweler and tell him you want to invest in a stone," he says "Tell him how much you want to spend — you'll have to talk in terms of thousands of dollars — and he'll say something to the effect that he'll see what he can find."

The jeweler, he explains, will then bring in on approval top stones from his suppliers. He has not had to pay for them. You decide on a stone. Let's say it's a diamond or an emerald priced at $5,000 cost. In a mounting, it would normally sell for $10,000 in the retailer's showcase, because it would have been in stock for some time and would have accumulated overhead. But because the stones are on approval, his selling cost is lower and he may retail it to you for $8,500.

"In 10 years," he adds, "if you put some work into selling that stone, and sell it the right way, you should get $14,000 for it, perhaps more. In a stable market, you should be able to make 8% a year. Although, in the past few years, the increases have been higher than that.

"When we make a sale like this, we often sell a mounting at cost so that the stone can be enjoyed in addition to being an investment. The best stones for investment are, in my opinion, diamond, emerald, ruby, sapphire and opal. But the investor likely to make the most money on a stone will always be the one who puts the most work into selling it."

And disposing of your stones does, if you bought from a retailer, entail more effort. In the gemstone business there is no established trading network such as exists for securities. As the vendor, you must approach potential purchasers: retailers, gemmological consultants, brokers and private collectors. And, of course, the greater the number of approaches you make, the higher the price you are likely to realize.

Your second route into the market is through the trade. Which means you'll become closely involved with stone dealers. That means you're going to have to do some homework.

A prominent Canadian gemmological consultant offers these guidelines for first-timers:

Don't rely on anyone but yourself for your research — you have to get deeply involved personally. Research the liquidity of precious stones by talking to jewelers and others in the trade. Talk to as many experts as possible. To find them, study the Yellow Pages.

Spend time studying precious stones, just as you would approach any other of your investments, and pay great attention to detail.

Take a portion of your investment capital that you feel you can afford to experiment with, and allot it to a gemstone program. Allow a portion of that allotment for research.

On the basis of research already done, make a purchase with a portion of your allotted capital. Then, immediately, turn around and try to sell the stone you've just purchased. The object of this exercise is to teach you the mechanics of trading.

You may fnd that you have difficulty reselling the stone. You may finally sell it for a short loss or a short profit. But now you know the stone has liquidity — and you've learned something about how the "club" operates. You've taken the first step towards becoming an enlightened gemstone investor.

Another approach worth considering if you have a lot of money to put into a gemstone portfolio is, according to this consultant, to hire a gemstone broker in whom you have confidence. Bear in mind though, a first-class broker demands first-class expenses: $500 a day for services, plus a brokerage fee of 3%-5%.

For this, he should be able to buy gemstones for you or to build a portfolio for you that, within a reasonable amount of time, you could liquidate at a substantial profit — say, 15% net. This, of course, would put your operation in the category of a real business. You would look on this broker in the same way as you would your accountant or lawyer.

Hiring a gemstone broker in this manner doesn't free you from the necessity of doing your own research and of experimenting on your own with buying and selling.

"I wouldn't consider gemstone investment without strong research," says the consultant. And that would include a detailed study of the different types of gems and their properties."

In fact, if there is one area of consensus among experts in the trade it is on the need for self-education on the part of new investors.

"You can be had very easily," says a colored-stone jewelry specialist who raises several flags on the matter of gemstone investing. "There are a number of pitfalls for the unwary. After you've studied up on gems, you should hire someone you trust implicitly as your broker.

"I've known retailers who have decided they're going to deal direct on their diamond buying instead of buying from their regular diamond dealer. And some of them were had. That's how they paid their dues in joining the club. When we as suppliers deal with stone people, we are dealing with established people who know the day-to-day prices with the cutters. Only on rare occasions do we deal directly with cutters."

Another flag: "When you get involved with bringing goods into Canada through a broker, you should remember that you are getting into a business and that you will have to thoroughly investigate the licensing situation as well as tax considerations. When we deal with anyone, we expect him to have the appro-

Some facts about gemstones

Gemstone	Color	Principal sources of supply	Comments
Emerald	Intense green	Colombia; Africa	Transparent; member of beryl family
Diamond	Colorless or very pale, steely blue	South Africa	Occasionally canary yellow, blue, green or pink
Ruby	Pigeon-blood red tending toward purple	Upper Burma; Thailand	Member of the corundum family along with sapphire; controversy as to how pale in color ruby may be before it is called a pink sapphire
Sapphire	Blue	Upper Burma; Thailand	Generally blue; can be any color but red
Aquamarine	Greenish blue	Brazil; Madagascar	Member of beryl family; more plentiful than emerald
Jade	White, green, beige, pink, mauve, gray	Burma; China	Identification of true jade is often difficult
Opal	White to blackish, with wide variety of internal colors	Australia; Mexico	Generally cut in a cabochon or other rounded shape to show colors; fragile
Pearl	Golden yellow, pink, white, creamy white	Natural: Persian Gulf; Gulf of Manaar. Cultured: Japan; South Seas	Though traditionally included in any description of gemstones is not actually a mineral
Peridot	Yellow green to deep bottle green	Burma; Island of Zebirget in Red Sea	Cleaves under excessive stress

Amethyst	Purple	Brazil	Occurs in wide range of colors; purple considered most desirable
Spinel	Wide variety of colors	Burma; Ceylon	Many historic rubies are actually red spinel; wide color range makes it resemble too many other gemstones
Topaz	Wine-yellow; orange yellow; blue; pink; brown and colorless. Mostly colorless	Brazil; Ceylon; Burma	Cleaves easily and markedly
Tourmaline	Wide color range	Mozambique; Madagascar; Brazil; Africa	Near emerald green color is popular; highly transparent; no tendency to cleave
Turquoise	Particular shade of blue	Nishapur district of Iran	Most is of inferior color and is treated to produce deeper color. Generally in cabochons, like opal; used for beads and carvings

priate license and documentation. The Mounties follow this sort of thing very carefully."

Diamonds have, of course, long been preeminent among precious stones — and their attraction rests on more than romantic appeal. They are, according to top gemmologist Eric Bruton's monograph *Diamonds*, a superb hedge against inflation:

"Prices of diamonds are kept stable. A stable average price means that as the cost of living goes up, so does the average price of diamonds. It means too that diamonds regarded as currency will purchase about the same now as they did last year, five years ago or 20 years ago . . . Compare this with the real value in purchasing power in most countries' paper money, which has plummeted. Diamonds are a good investment if they are of top quality and are large enough. In practice, this means the best stones to invest in are from one to three carats in weight and of River, VVSI (very, very slight inclusion) quality or better."

Qualities that go into making a stone a gemstone are many, but there are three major requirements: (1) it must be of appealing color and lustre or sheen; (2) it must not be of common occurrence; and (3) it must be sufficiently hard and tough to withstand wear over long periods.

There is always a good chance that you may become so fascinated with the lustre and sparkle of your stones that you decide to invest for the long haul and become a collector. In that case you'd do well to abide by the paramount guiding principle that applies to all collections:

Reject inferior specimens; buy only the very best stones you can afford. Admit only gems of the finest quality and largest size to your collection. High-grade collections are more readily marketed.

You can, of course, employ either of the market approaches mentioned earlier. But it is often a good idea to confide your plans to a trusted trade member, and have him act as your broker. He can acquire gems to suit your requirements from a wide variety of sources — trade level, auctions, other collectors, estate jewelry, secondhand outlets, and jewelers in other countries.

Adequate insurance coverage for your collection is important too. Prices of some stones change frequently. Which means the replacement cost of your collection is constantly increasing. So you'll have to have it reappraised regularly by an expert capable of determining the replacement value of each stone.

To further protect your collection, lodge it with your bank or in your stone broker's safe. And be sure to keep adequate records that include the following particulars of each stone: Its variety name, color and carat weight; its shape and style of cutting; the locality of its origin; from whom it was acquired and date of acquisition; price paid and estimated current value; and its notable characteristics, such as inclusions, particulars of its history, and unusual physical properties.

More than 2,000 minerals make up the earth's crust, but only a minute fraction of these qualify as gemstones. And when really fine gemstones are considered, the available amount shrinks even further.

10

Some basic rules
for buying diamonds

Unless you happen to be in the late King Edward VII's position of having the nine Cullinan diamonds (total: 1,055.99 carats) presented to you, or of being the heir to the vast, gorgeous crown jewels of Iran — and thus unworried, basically, about their market worth — be careful how, where, and from whom you buy a diamond.

As an investment, diamonds leave something to be desired; over the last 20 years or so, any good blue chip would have served you better. As a hedge against devaluation, or political vicissitudes, they've been pretty good — especially if, as victim of a *coup d'etat*, the owner has to leave in a hurry in the middle of the night.

Less melodramatically, diamonds can certainly be used to complement securities, real estate and art in a wealthy person's portfolio. We emphasize wealthy because, not only are diamonds a long-term investment paying no dividends (decoration aside), but they have to be substantial in size, and of top quality, to be sure of accruing in value.

By virtue of their rarity, gems of more than five carats are bound to increase in value, especially if flawless in color and clarity. Certainly, according to experts in the field, no stone under one-carat is of investment grade. Diamonds ranging from 10-point (10% of a carat) to around three-quarter-carat — though undoubtedly effective in getting her to say yes, or even maybe — are the staple of the retail trade, where taxes and markups are built-in, and thus hopeless from an investment viewpoint.

(A carat is the unit of weight used for precious stones. One carat equals three grains or 200 milligrams — or about six thousandths of an ounce.)

When we asked one cutter-importer to sum up the problems the would-be investor might face, he did so in one word: *marketability*. The diamond trade is simply not set up for the amateur. It lacks the instant liquidity of the stock market.

There are no public quotations for the price of gems. The general secrecy — almost an air of conspiracy — that seems to surround the small, exclusive world of diamond traders leaves little room for the outsider. To speculate, and speculate successfully, one would have to be very rich indeed — rich enough to wait, perhaps for years, until the right buyer turns up to buy that rare, expensive stone.

For obviously the price of such a stone only becomes a price when someone is willing to pay it; in other words, it takes not only patience, but substantial resources, to be able to realize the full potential of a costly stone. In Canada such a waiting game hardly makes sense. For one thing, the right psychological climate doesn't exist — the ingrained instinct for conspiracy and the sudden *putsch*, midnight jackboots and the hurried flight across the border.

And then, more prosaically, the tax on diamonds is a real deterrent: 22% excise duty and federal tax, plus whatever slice the province might take, say 5%, which is built into the price of a diamond by the time it reaches the retail level. Thus, the owner could not expect to re-sell at a profit to a dealer — whose license gaves him exemption from excise and federal taxes when *he* imports from his supplier. In addition, finding a private buyer (unless the stone is truly exceptional) entails the usual complications, among them persuading a buyer to pay provincial tax twice on the same article.

Canadian investors can get around this tax obstacle quite legally by buying abroad, and never importing the stone(s). Instead, they rent a safety deposit box in a European bank until they are ready to re-sell.

Experts say that illegal traffic in diamonds is quite sizable. A knowledgable estimate puts the value of gems smuggled into this country at as high as 40% of official figures on legal imports.

If selling diamonds sounds discouraging, just wait till you get to the buying. Unless you're very well advised — and even if you are — the risks are considerable. Not only may you overpay for the genuine article, but you may simply not be aware of the fine nuances that distinguish clarity, cut and color in the grading of diamonds.

Even practised gemmologists assess stones under special conditions: northern light, preferably before noon, and then only after looking at stones for half an hour or so to sharpen the faculties.

The finest color, of course, is no color at all, a flawless transparency; the faintest blue tint is also highly prized. But where a pink, lilac, green, brandy-brown or yellow shading is evident — classified by De Beers as "fancy class" — the price is correspondingly lower. Such shadings are always measured against a standard colorless stone.

Mark Gross, a Toronto cutter and wholesaler, told a story that nicely illustrates this point. He and his new bride took their honeymoon trip to London, where they were invited to the home of a famous and very wealthy diamond dealer. After dinner, the old gentleman went to a safe and brought out a magnificent 20-carat diamond, which glittered on the white tablecloth.

Mark Gross and his young wife oohed and aahed at the flawless gem. With a smile, their host produced another 20-carat diamond and place it next to the first one, which, in comparison, looked somewhat less than perfect; definitely yellow beside its colorless neighbor. More oohs and aahs. But now came a third 20-carat stone, which had the effect, clearly, of devaluing the first two with *its* perfection. It was only at the fifth 20-carat diamond that their owner admitted true flawlessness. Beside it, the four formerly splendid gems, in descending order, looked all right, so-so, inferior and downright tawdry.

The perfect stone, of whatever size, has no spots, "feathers," fractures or other tiny inclusions in it. The internal reflections of the facets sometimes have the effect of obscuring a real flaw, at other times of magnifying an insignificant imperfection. Such stones are classified as "pique goods," and, in combination with

82

factors of color, cut, and size, put the stone within a fairly predictable price range.

The cut of a diamond strongly influences its marketability. To avoid the vagaries of fashion, it is best to select a style that hasn't changed much over the years, such as the "American" or "Marquis" cut (the latter adding as much as 10% to the price), rather than the oval, emerald, pear or heart-shaped cuts, which seem old-fashioned to modern eyes.

Speaking technically, the proportion of the facets has a lot to do with the effect of a stone. A Toronto gemmologist, Jonathan Fraleigh, sums it up this way: "A fine diamond must have identical facets; at the corners, each facet must meet its neighbor exactly. The girdle — neither too thin nor too wide — must have no rough spots. A diamond cut either too deep or too shallow below the girdle will let light escape through the angled facets, and so lose fire and brilliancy. It will be worth less per carat."

Now to the crucial question of size. All things being equal, the size of a diamond largely determines its worth. The *rarity* of quality diamonds above, say, eight to 10 carats, puts them in a class of their own. Their annual rate of appreciation — assuming always the existence of a buyer — is certainly higher, and will become even more so in the future, than the more common one-carat stone.

Since that assumption can't always be made, it's safe to say that the smaller stone becomes the better investment, since buyers do exist at this level. Indeed, probably the best buy in terms of instant liquidity (and therefore of high annual appreciation) is the poor, medium-grade, one-carat stone which almost trebled in value in five years. Not much, perhaps, compared to high flyers in the stock market, but neither such painful nosedives in bad times. Steady is the word.

But the size-cost relationship is not an arithmetical one; up to a certain level it's exponential, and then flattens out. Thus, a one-carat diamond might be worth, say, $4,000-$4,500; the same quality two-carat stone would then fetch around $12,000; three carats might reach $19,000; at five carats, a buyer might have to go as high as $9,000 per carat.

Finally, Elizabeth Taylor's highly publicized bauble weighing in at 69 carats, valued in the early 1970s at $1 million, priced out at just over $15,000 per carat. If her husband, Richard Burton, had even higher ambitions, he probably wouldn't have had to pay a higher *rate*.

Just more dollars for more carats.

To sum up then. An investor should never put himself into the position of being pressed to liquidate his stones; buyers of the high-voltage stuff aren't too common these days. But, given patience and good contacts, the biggest potential profit is in stones of five to eight carats.

For quick, easy marketability — especially in Canada — the three-quarter-carat to one-carat, medium-quality stone is probably best, even though the increment will be smaller. Antwerp is where you go if you're a serious buyer, but take along a trusted expert, and make sure you have good northern light. With a hundred or two hundred thousand to spend, you're likely to get fairly courteous attention.

If, on the other hand, you have other problems on your mind, like how to pay the bills, diamonds are not for you — not for investment anyway. To adorn a loved one it will pay you to go to a reputable jeweler.

The gain is likely to be under 100% on smaller stones, but at least you'll avoid the confidential deal through a cousin of a cousin that ends up being so expensive.

After all, how do you complain to a cousin of a cousin that that flawless stone seems to have a yellowish cloud in it, speckled with black dots, and cut with the symmetry of a pat of butter . . .

Amsterdam has always been *the* diamond-cutting centre, with New York a close second. In recent years, though, Israel has moved up strongly.

The world's leading primary sources of rough, uncut gems are still, of course, South Africa, South-West Africa and the Congo (about 32 million carats, of gem and industrial grades). Russia is estimated to mine about 3½ million carats, and various South American countries just short of one million carats.

Unlike securities markets, where prices find their own levels in the ebb and flow of supply and demand, the diamond market is fairly rigidly controlled. De Beers Consolidated Mines, representing a tightly knit group of producing mines like Premier, Dutoitspan, Wesselton and Jagersfontein in the Kimberley, Orange Free State and Transvaal regions of South Africa, controls the sale and distribution of about 80% of the world's output; this includes Russia, which finds it convenient to profit from De Beers' immense expertise in the field.

The company's accurate grading system, plus the financial resources to set prices — and make them stick — makes the diamond business the orderly, generally predictable, and close-mouthed fraternity that it is.

Two or three times a year, De Beers' Diamond Trading Co. arranges "sightings," to which cutters from most countries are invited. Parcels of uncut gems, assembled by size and shape, are made up according to the specifications of customers. Big stones, individually priced, are subject to a certain amount of discreet haggling; smaller stones of less brilliant potential are on a take-it-or-leave-it basis, though more than two or three leave-its are liable to cut off any future invitations to "sightings."

According to one Toronto gem cutter, Mark Gross, of S. Gross & Son Diamonds Ltd., a very special expertise is needed on these occasions. But not only expertise; also gut instinct. Though he may handle, peer, tap and sniff the uncut stones, the customer has no absolute way of knowing what may lie at the heart of the diamond; only the final polishing will reveal its precise color, whether it has microscopic flaws or inclusions or internal fractures.

Any of these will drastically reduce the price, as compared to the colorless and flawless stone. Here, then, is where the real risk lies — buying at the rough stage. Once its 58 facets have been cut, the stone becomes a known quantity, subject only to human circumstances — the love of show, fear for the future, the magpie's instinct to hoard, an urge to express love.

Or, as many a deposed dictator has found, the most compact form of transporting a looted treasury known to man.

The rapid appreciation in the value of jewelry in recent years has left many Canadian gem owners seriously under-insured.

"The value of some stones has increased 5%-6% a year in the past; in some cases there have been increases of 15% in a short period," Hugh Proctor, Hugh Proctor & Co., Toronto, diamond dealers and appraisers, says. Insurance agents and brokers are urging their clients to have precious items of jewelry appraised at least on each policy anniversary, which is usually every three years. Some insurance companies now make appraisals mandatory every three years on all items insured for $500 or more.

Gemmologists say there are two main reasons for the jump in gem values:

1. Growing demand for quality stones. Prosperity in Japan and Europe has put many more people in a position to buy diamonds and other precious stones (mainly emeralds, sapphires and rubies).

2. Availability of good-quality synthetic stones, which sell for about one third the price of real stones, has actually increased interest in the real thing. In recent years companies such as Union Carbide Co. have developed processes for growing synthetic emeralds and rubies which are very hard to tell from real stones.

The growth in gem values has left many owners who have lost jewelry or had it stolen sadly disappointed when they come to replace it. "A fine quality stone of one or two carats and over can increase in value by one third over a three-year policy period," Proctor says. "This means a stone insured for $3,000 when the policy is issued could easily be worth $4,000 when the policy is due for renewal."

For all-risks coverage on jewelry, the three-year insurance rate is 4% of the value. If the jewelry is included as part of a policy covering a house, contents and personal liability (homeowners policy), this rate is usually reduced by 10%.

Cost of having jewelry appraised varies widely, depending on what type it is. For a single-stone ring, the fee may run close to $15. When several items are involved, the gemmologist usually charges on a time basis.

11

About using Canada's own death-tax havens

The federal government stepped out of death duties when it repealed the Estate Tax Act. Some provinces promptly moved into the succession-duty field, while some chose to become death-tax havens. Your place of residence at the time of death can make a big difference to your heirs — and so can the "place of residence" of a company set up to hold your assets.

The "situs" of shares of a company, particularly a private company, can have a major effect on death taxes exerted by some of the provinces, despite the repeal of the Estate Tax Act.

(Situs, incidentally, is the legal location as opposed to the physical location. These may or may not coincide.)

The details relating to place and register for transfer of shares should be carefully documented, particularly if a provincial tax haven is being used.

Take the case of Eli Prelutsky vs The Queen. While the Prelutsky case was under the Estate Tax Act, it was the register of transfers and place of transfer that was at issue.

The deceased was the beneficial owner of all the shares of the capital stock of a private corporation incorporated in Saskatchewan. In 1941, the deceased moved from Saskatchewan to British Columbia and lived there until his death in 1971.

In 1955, the company was registered as an extra-provincial company in British Columbia under the B.C. Company Act.

Thereafter, the company had no assets in Saskatchewan, carried on no business there, and had its head office in British Columbia, although at all times it maintained a registered office in Saskatchewan.

In 1958 and in 1970, transfers of shares took place. In each case, the minutes of meetings in British Columbia approving the transfers were prepared in British Columbia, were retained in the company's minute book, and notations of the transfers were made on the share-certificate stubs in the share-certificate book. The minute book and stubs had been kept in British Columbia since 1941 and never returned to Saskatchewan, and the minute book contained a sheet headed "Register of shareholders" that contained information on transfers.

At that time, the company had no book entitled "Register of Transfers," and neither the law of British Columbia nor Saskatchewan required the keeping of a register of transfers or a place of transfer. Both provinces required corporations to keep a register of members with particulars of any transfer of shares, and such register was to be kept at the registered office of the corporation.

In computing tax payable under the Estate Tax Act, the minister disallowed a provincial tax credit for British Columbia duties on the ground that the shares were situated in Saskatchewan — since, contrary to the act, the company kept no register of transfers and had no place of transfer in British Columbia under Section 9 of the act where the deceased was domiciled.

The estate appealed and the credit was allowed.

The judge found that the function of a register of transfers and the reason for a place of transfer were simply to facilitate dealing in shares. The terms "register of transfers or place of transfer" were not defined in the Estate Tax Act. In the case of a private company, even less formality was required, provided the corporate statutory requirements were met. The records maintained in British Columbia were sufficient to constitute the maintenance of "register of transfer" and the head office in British Columbia was a "place of transfer" for the company's shares in that province since it had no business in Saskatchewan, and it was registered in British Columbia and maintained records there.

The judge held that the shares of the company were situated in British Columbia for the purposes of the Estate Tax Act, and the minister's assessment was set aside. The amount at stake in this matter was more than $400,000 of federal estate tax.

For many years, individuals have attempted to shift the situs of their assets from one jurisdiction to another, usually from a taxing jurisdiction to a tax haven. In the past, this has usually entailed removing assets from Canada. But under our present provincial legislation, the only provinces levying death taxes are British Columbia, Saskatchewan, Manitoba, Ontario and Quebec, and consequently the other provinces have become tax havens. Of these, Alberta has been the most widely publicized.

While mere shifting of situs does not necessarily achieve a tax saving, it is of prime importance that when a company is incorporated in a tax haven to hold an individual's assets, all steps must be taken to ensure that the situs is secure. Eli Prelutsky was successful for the taxpayer, but the decision hinged on details of compliance, place of transfer, and register of transfer.

The detail is of the utmost importance to ensure that the residence of the corporation in the haven can be satisfactorily upheld. Management and control should be exercised effectively where the company is legally situated, not from elsewhere.

Some of the important steps to follow are:

— Head office and only place of transfer should be located in the nontaxing province.

— All directors and shareholders meetings should be held in the nontaxing province.

— A trust agreement should be set up with residents of the nontaxing province as trustees to provide the legal shareholding requirements, and a board of directors who are residents of the province should be established.

— Conform carefully to the provincial requirements for filing returns, etc., and these should be prepared in that province.

— All meetings and minutes held in that province should be properly and carefully documented at all times.

The Prelutsky case in 1974, the Leckie case in 1967, and the Schiller Estate case in 1969 all related to the difficult question of situs of shares, which is one of the primary grounds of provincial death duty. Consequently, where situs is being shifted or established elsewhere, it is evident from those cases that the detail in setting up a holding company is of vital and prime importance.

12

Behind the furor over government annuities

If you're one of the 270,000-odd Canadians now paying into or collecting from a federal-government annuity contract, you're probably sorry you ever got involved.

If you're not and if you or an employer are thinking about getting you newly involved now — think again.

The earnings on contributions to a government annuity plan aren't competitive with those in private plans. Despite this, a few trusting souls each year have insisted on buying from Ottawa.

They can't anymore, because all *new* sales of government annuities have been discontinued. However, *employers* who have existing contracts with the government will be able to register new employees until March 31, 1979. If you're planning to switch jobs, you should ask about this.

Although the government annuities branch has done very little new business since 1967, it continues to make news. Scarcely a month goes by without questions in the House of Commons. Many of the questions are prompted by pleas from MPs' constituents, some of whom have written directly to the government and the annuities branch.

The government recently gave in to this pressure and almost doubled the rate of return on its annuities from a dismal 4% to a still uncompetitive 7% — and that was a sharp departure from hard-line government policy.

The federal finance minister had previously refused to make any increase in the annuity rates despite repeated entreaties from those receiving annuity payments and those paying into annuity plans. But then, with no reference to his previous stance, he boosted the rate of return on existing government annuities.

The 7% rate is an improvement, but, by contrast, contributions made to a private insurance-company annuity recently were earning about 9%. Up until the 1950s, the rate guaranteed under the government annuity plans was very competitive with that offered by insurance companies. In recent years, however, the fixed government rates have been badly out of line with those of the insurance companies.

Those collecting annuity payments had asked the government to adjust the interest rate so that their payments could be increased to mitigate the effects of inflation. Those paying into an annuity plan had pointed out that they could do far better putting their money elsewhere.

The government won't permit cash withdrawals under its annuity plan; if you don't like the rates, all you can do is stop making payments into the plan.

The low rates available under the government plans had cut the sales of new government annuities recently to about 20 contracts a year. Since 1967, the government hadn't been actively promoting the sale of its annuities, and had been advising applicants that the government rates were no longer competitive with those offered by insurance companies. Now all new sales have been stopped.

Pleas and complaints have been pouring in not only from those receiving annuity payments (annuitants) who want the government to increase the fixed payout to help ease the effects of inflation, but also from those making regular monthly or yearly contributions toward an annuity. The contributors want to be able to withdraw the money they've contributed and deposit it elsewhere at a higher yield than it earns in the government annuity account.

The government's decisions to raise the yield on Canada Savings Bonds held to maturity, and adjust the Canada Pension Plan, Old Age Security and civil service pension plans in order to provide increases in accordance with rises in the consumer price index, fueled the argument for boosting the annuity payouts.

The actual annuity amount paid to a particular annuitant is the amount he contracted for when he signed up for an annuity, and the maximum payout under the government program is $100 a month.

For a long time the government turned a deaf ear to the pleas. Then, however, it made a concession to inflation. Those who collect their annuity before they become eligible for Old Age Security or Canada Pension Plan payments may, on request, have their annuity payment increased beyond the $100 maximum. These increases are designed to help retired people in the transition period between age 60, say, and age 65 when they receive OAS and CPP benefits. At age 65, a downward adjustment is made in the government annuity payment to compensate for the higher payments made prior to age 65.

The government stoutly resisted any further adjustments until it did its surprise about-turn and raised the annuity rate to 7%. But it firmly refused to permit those who are contributing to an annuity to withdraw their money and put it elsewhere. So, if you're in, you're stuck in.

Officials in the finance minister's office say that not everyone who is collecting a government annuity is a hardship case. Furthermore, they say it is a false analogy to equate annuities with Canada Savings Bonds. The bonds may be cashed at any time, where annuities are a long-term investment. (And with 19 annuitants 100 years old or more on the government's books, the payout period can be quite prolonged, too.)

Cash withdrawals are out of the question, the government says, because an annuity is a contract; the buyers knew what they were getting and should be willing to abide by the terms. The government stresses that it will stick to its commitment to pay the full annuity — even if interest rates take a big tumble.

Under the government scheme, the guaranteed rate credited to the annuitant's account is, in effect, the same as the rate of interest the government assumes it can earn on its money. But the annuities branch really doesn't earn anything on the money. The 7%, or whatever, is merely a bookkeeping rate; the contributions made to the annuity plans are not invested in anything.

Herein lies the big difference between the government annuity plan and the annuities sold by insurance companies. The insurance companies base their annuity rates, in large part, on what they can earn on the money in the market. (Expenses and the mortality rate are other factors.) The life firms recently were using interest-rate assumptions of around 9%. (The insurance company hopes to make a return by earning more than it guarantees.)

The gap in the rates had discouraged all but a few from buying from the government. A handful — about 20 people a year — were still buying from the government up until new sales were stopped. The annuities branch says those few were often people who'd had some bad experience with private investments and trusted only the government.

These small numbers were a far cry from the booming sales in the late 1930s, through to the 1950s, when the interest rate guaranteed by the government program was very competitive with that offered by the insurance companies. In 1947, the record sales year, 9,530 individual deferred annuity contracts and 3,644 individual immediate annuities were sold, and 30,411 individual certificates were issued under group pension plan contracts.

At the close of the annuities branch's fiscal year on March 31, 1974, payouts were being made under 124,744 individual contracts and pension plan certificates. Total payout was $74 million. Revenue, including "interest" of $50 million on the $1.3-billion assets and premium income of $6 million, was just over $56 million.

The annuities branch estimates that by the year 2030, almost all of the annuity contracts will have matured and the annuitants will be collecting their payments. The fund will likely have disappeared by then. But unless the government has disappeared too, the fund's demise won't affect continuation of the annuity payments.

13

The horse as earner: your stable-floor tips

Klitos Argyrides and six other Greek restaurateurs bought their first thoroughbred racer in 1961 and set up Hellenic Stables. Nothing much happened until they acquired another horse called All Canadian — an E. P. Taylor cast-off — for $2,500. All Canadian went on to earn about $64,000. Hellenic Stables is firmly in the black.

Jim Shaw of Ancaster, Ontario, owns a trotting filly, Shawland Belle. Of her 11 races in 1974, she won eight and placed second in two, picking up $83,521 for Shaw.

The horse — man's best investment in these troubled financial times?

Well no, not necessarily. For every Cinderella story in the racing business, there are 100 losers. Less than 38% of those who invest in horseflesh manage to break even.

Consider, for instance, the case of Bill Livingston, president of Sovereign General Assurance and Sovereign Life Assurance Co. of Canada. Livingston and his fellow-members in an investment club learned a $3,500 lesson when they purchased a thoroughbred yearling for that price as part of their portfolio. The horse started 10 times and performed disastrously 10 times. They bailed out and Livingston says, "Never again!"

Then there's Clarence Graham of Woodbridge, Ontario, who breeds, trains and shows his hackney ponies. For him, horses are an expensive hobby. A good hackney, he says, is worth $4,000-$6,000, yet show-ring purses — and his highsteppers do collect a lot of prizes — often aren't much larger than $100.

Three Toronto stockbrokers, Len Andrews, George Atkins and Ray Slingerland, started up Canbay Stables with a thoroughbred brood mare bought for $750. Last year they raced a filly and colt which earned them around $11,000 in prize money. They're just breaking even and, if they haven't exactly conquered the racing world, they console themselves that they've adhered to their original intention, which was to have fun.

Whatever the reasons for investing in horseflesh, it's a tricky business and no easy way to make money. In many ways it's like the stock market, with infinite variables to consider, not the least of which is the fact that you're dealing with a live, temperamental and extremely risky commodity.

But, no matter how it ranks as an investment, the horse business is currently a booming one. In Canada alone it's a $2-billion-a-year industry and our exploding national equine population is already far larger than it was in the days when the horse was our chief means of transportation. Not only that, the variety of breeds represented in Canada is increasing by leaps and bounds each year.

And while owning a horse is obviously no sure way to make a million, breeding can be a good long-term investment, according to an article published in Barron's in 1972 which concluded, "A man can build up his herd and land during his years of peak income and, by retirement, theoretically, is ready to reap the rewards."

Certainly, the big money is in breeding. Big racing stables such as Windfields (thoroughbreds) and ABC Farms (standardbreds) readily allow that their dollars come from breeding, not racing. Large operations like these, too, are generally subsidiaries of holding companies and are able to move their profits around. If you *do* make big prize money at racing, most horse people will advise you, the smart thing to do is put your winnings into buying another horse, thus burying your gains, since the maximum tax writeoff an owner (or part-owner) in Canada can claim is $5,000 per horse.

Returns on breeding both pleasure and race horses can be

substantial. Top Arab stallion Serenity Ibn Nazir commands a $5,000 stud fee. (His own price would be upwards of $100,000 if he were for sale.) For race horses, stud fees are at an all-time high. Trotters reportedly command fees of up to $15,000; the best thoroughbred stallions may go as high as $50,000 — and they are available only to breeders who have already paid heavily to own a piece of them through a syndicate. (Secretariat is syndicated at $6.5 million.)

Indeed, with the strong likelihood of legalized off-track betting, with the mushrooming of racetracks all across the country, and with a total annual purse already worth more than $40 million, breeding race horses may look very attractive.

But can it all hold up? Obviously, judging from the long lines of buyers at the yearling sales, many people believe so. And while outsiders, measuring the incredible horse market against the rest of an economy that lacks meat and fuel and stock profits, may attribute it all to sheer madness, the insiders have history on their side; the racing business has tended to thrive in times of recession and depression.

Before you rush out, chequebook in hand, to take part in the gamble of horse ownership, however, there are many points to ponder. Raising horses is a specialized business and one that novices frequently waltz into all too lightly; one prominent breeder says that she has known only one buyer who took the common-sense precaution of bringing a vet with him to check his prospective purchase. And diseases like equine infectious anaemia, screw worm and even influenza can spell disaster for a whole stable.

Ponder the fact that your investment is a highly sensitive and intelligent creature. Racehorses have been known to go into severe depressions after losing. Pleasure horses sometimes use their wits to make life difficult for their owners. For example, there's the case of one Arab whose owner ran an electrified wire around his stall in an attempt to foil his habit of seeking attention by tearing down buckets, feedbags and anything else on the walls; the horse quickly learned how to check whether the current was on with one whisker before tearing the wire down too.

Ponder the possibility of accidents. An accident may, in seconds, reduce the value of your investment from $50,000 to about $500.

Ponder, if breeding is in your mind, the very low fertility rate for mares. Only 40%-50% of mares are able to conceive, and that only 40%-50% of pregnant mares produce live offspring. And, no matter how good your stallion, if he doesn't get mares that produce good offspring, *his* value rapidly declines.

Last but not least, you will of course have to ponder the great variety of breeds available. Costs of getting in and chances of making a profit vary considerably from breed to breed, as you'll see from the six examples covered later in this chapter.

Nor do those six represent the total spectrum of possibilities for the horse buyer. There are also the "western" pleasure-horse breeds — Pintos, Appaloosas, Palominos, Paints. They're all selling well here. Or you may go esoteric and opt for a Morgan or a Tennessee Walking Horse. The first is a small, chunky all-round type, the second a breed with very sloping hindquarters, originally developed on southern plantations. Even these relatively rare mounts are now being bred in Canada.

Whatever breed you choose, once you have taken possession of your four-legged investment, you'll probably never be the same again. Horse people *are* different. And no matter whether their purchase was made with a view to enchancing their egos or their bank balances, there's the unavoidable impression that their decision to invest in horseflesh was an emotional rather than a rational one.

And, of course, they're all gamblers. A great horse is not merely a product of careful breeding, expert training and tender loving care. A great horse, as the breeders will tell you, is an act of God.

Here are the basic facts about some of the breeds popular in Canada.

Arabians:
"Who needs racing?" says Ray Wilkins, a top breeder and trainer of Arabs. The whole racing scene — syndicated ownership of top sires with prices rising and falling like a yo-yo depending on how their offspring do at the track — is not for her. She points

out that, whereas the cost of keeping a race horse in training is around $6,500 a year, you can train an Arab for showing for $200 a month, and stabling and feeding a pleasure horse costs around $100 per month.

Among pleasure horses, Arabs are one of the most aristocratic breeds — and one of the hottest on the market. They're often bought by people who fall for their undoubted beauty and fabled history. However, Ms Wilkins says, they're also falling for the most intelligent breed. And the one with the greatest stamina: "In the U.S. they hold 100-mile races and only Arabs have the endurance for them."

You'll pay dearly for this paragon — not less than $3,000 for a good one, Ms Wilkins suggests.

Quarters:

Fastest-growing pleasure breed right now is the quarter horse. If you like the certain masculine image that goes with riding western style, this one is for you. The quarter horse shares with the Arab the advantage of being easy to train. But you can get in more reasonably; a good horse will cost you around $1,000. And you're buying a versatile mount; in addition to pleasure riding, the breed is famous for roping, cutting — and producing the fastest quarter-mile racers in the world. So you may have a racer on your hands too (they start at around $2,500), and indeed quarter-horse racing is becoming popular in Canada with purses already up to $7,000.

Hunters:

"Hunter classics are mushrooming all across the country," points out Tom Gayford of the Canadian equestrian team. Gayford claims that hunting and show jumping are not the exclusive preserves of the rich. For as little as $500 you can buy a good hunter or maybe a thoroughbred which isn't going to prove out at the track, train it yourself and compete in shows with quite lucrative purses. If you've got a winner, the price may go sky-high; a top jumper may command $150,000. And they are scarce — the equestrian team, Gayford says, goes all over the place to find good mounts, including "begging, borrowing and stealing them from friends."

Gayford himself started small and hit lucky — with a gelding

98

of unremarkable parentage which his father had raised and which went on to win the Governor General's Colt Cup and to become U.S. Champion Hunter before taking an Olympic gold medal.

Hunter/jumper people are generally already into horse breeding, have come up via the pony club, and often appear to enjoy their hobby as much for the social life it spawns as for riding itself.

Ponies:

If you want to get in with next to nothing — and risk coming out with next to nothing — you need a pony. The bottom has dropped out of the pony market. Unless you breed one with blue-chip bloodlines you can hardly give it away; in fact one breeder recently did give away his entire herd because it was costing him too much to feed.

But who knows, maybe there'll be a turnaround and you'll make a killing; not long before prices hit rock bottom, a black pony stallion named Frisco Pete sold in the U.S. for a remarkable $65,000.

Dressage:

Maybe you're interested in breeding equine ballet dancers. "The classical art of dressage," says Ed Rothkranz, a Canadian advanced dressage champion, "is going up 100% every year. Olympic dressage can cost you a fortune — six years at least to train your horse with training fees alone at $400 a month. But for the low-level dressage rider, it's inexpensive. You can do it after only a few lessons, and it's a wonderful obedience training for any horse — hunter, jumper, thoroughbred, even quarter horse."

Good dressage horses are as rare in Canada as good show jumpers. Rothkranz says. (He is the only top Canadian dressage rider to breed and train his own horse.) That situation should change before too long, though, now that we have Lipizzaners on Canadian soil.

Lipizzaners — the ancient and beautiful breed of white horses made famous by the Spanish Riding School in Vienna — are dressage horses par excellence. Five years ago, Ian Munro, executive vice-president of Four Seasons Hotels Ltd. and his wife Marcia brought the first Lipizzaner to Canada. They now have four brood mares, a stallion and six colts and are in the process of putting together a 12-member syndicate — first ever for this intelligent, aristocratic, all-round breed.

Drafts:
Presenting a fairly healthy investment picture are draft horses. Paul Durish owns 20 tons of draft horse and says it's showing a profit.

Durish, millionaire-entrepreneur owner of Durish Investments Ltd. (which in turn owns farm-equipment manufacturer McKee Brothers Ltd.) bought 19 Belgians — blond giants which weigh 2,400 pounds apiece and stand a massive 19 hands tall — to promote his products, at a cost of $100,000. Price for draft horses have risen at least 50% over the past couple of years, according to journals of the trade. A good Belgian, Clydesdale or Percheron now costs at least $5,000.

Another healthy sign: demand for draft horses exceeds supply. If you're squeamish, however, you shouldn't inquire too closely into one of the reasons for this. The big drafts have proven to be the best breed for the PMU (pregnant mares' urine) farms which produce estrogen for birth-control pills and where methods are not likely to gladden the hearts of genuine animal lovers.

If, having chosen your breed, you would like names and addresses of owners and breeders in your area, write Canadian National Livestock Records, 2417 Holly Lane, Ottawa K1V 7P2.

If you'd like a little more expertise in horseflesh, many local community colleges have courses in equine studies. One of the best is a two-year diploma course run by Humber College, Toronto — which, significantly, reports that 90% of course graduates have no problem finding employment in the burgeoning world of the horse.

14

Some expert views
on art investment

Why was John Marion, president and chief auctioneer of Sotheby Parke Bernet, New York, talking about fine art to a group of Canadian investors?

Very simple. In times when stocks have taken a beating, when currencies are relatively unstable, even in some of the most highly industrialized countries in the world, there is always a tendency to look for something more solid than equity or currency.

Citing the unstable conditions in Europe in the 1930s, Marion said that a great many people then put their money into what was "available, salable, and portable."

Many very good pictures came out of Europe in the 1930s sewn inside the lining of people's overcoats. Small sculptures were somehow handled across the borders, and, of course, jewelry, which is relatively easy to hide, was the basis on which a great many refugees took the decision to leave and try their luck in less repressive countries than those in which they were born.

Marion was not, however, equating the 1970s with the 1930s. What he was doing was showing that at any time when a currency shows weakness, art objects are one of the alternative methods of conserving real wealth. But it also happens when a currency is strong. Then it is because the strength of the buying currency means the price in the selling country is at a discount.

Recently, for example, when the Japanese currency was very

strong, there was a great deal of buying by the Japanese at any one of the seven auction rooms Marion's company operates in London, New York, Toronto, Zurich, and Amsterdam. But the Japanese then disappeared from the market and they were replaced temporarily by buyers from Portugal who were trying to head off any currency restrictions that might apply after the political upset in that country.

Then, Marion said, it was the Italians who were buying — not because their currency was strong, but because it was weak and the whole economic situation in Italy was precarious.

What were they buying? Well, the Japanese bought a lot of French impressionist paintings, inflating prices for Renoir, Dégas and Cézanne to more than $200,000 for a mediocre picture and more than $1 million for very good ones.

They also bought Chinese porcelain — and Marion reminded his audience that one collector had paid $1 million for a blue-and-white vase. That raised a question from a member of the audience: "What does one do with a blue-and-white jar that cost $1 million?" Though Marion did not answer directly, the orthodox answer is, of course: you keep it until you can sell it for $1.25 million which may well happen within the next five years.

That is why Marion was in Canada. He was talking about the acquisition of art objects as an investment, and, as recent figures show, the appreciation in the value of art is at an annual rate of 20%.

Marion was there to discuss, in fact, how to go about acquiring art.

What are the rules?

The first and cardinal rule: buy quality.

"You don't look for bargains in the stock market unless you are a real pro (and even then you may be wrong), and you certainly won't find them in the art market as an amateur," Marion said.

If you are thinking of either acquiring art through dealers or through the auction rooms, you must get just as good investment counsel as you would if you were putting your money anywhere else.

The reason why some buyers do not do this is that art is to be looked at as well as kept as an investment. So subjective decisions are made on the basis of what a picture will look like hanging, instead of an objective decision depending on what it will fetch five years from now in the sale room.

The second thing Marion made clear was that all Sotheby sales are not in the million-dollar category. In fact, a great majority of its sales are in the $500-$700 range.

"The trouble with the press reporting our sales is that they look either for sensationally high prices or newsworthy buyers rather than giving an account of the whole sale," Marion said. "In the same sale that we sold a diamond for $1 million to Richard Burton for Elizabeth Taylor, we sold a lot of other jewelry which was not nearly in that category, but neither the recipients nor the buyers were noticed."

But is there a real art market in the sense that there is a market for stocks? Marion affirmed there certainly is. He said that his firm is the leading auctioneer of art and art objects in the world; that Christie's and others also have very successful sale rooms; that the annual cash value of works changing hands in the past few years has been in the neighborhood of $1 billion.

There is no question that if you buy a good Renoir today, you can sell it very easily any time in the next five or 10 years. Also, the documentation that has to be provided about where it comes from, its authenticity, and its ownership history are all listed in the sale catalogues. Furthermore, every Sotheby's sale has an estimated price (by each entry in the catalogue) as a sort of bench mark.

The circulation of these catalogues to every major dealer and other auction houses in the world also prevents stolen material from getting onto the market easily. Recently, in fact, Marion's own auction room in New York withdrew 30 lots a European dealer had spotted as stolen property.

There is, however, a danger resulting from the circulation of such catalogues as well as the beneficial effect just referred to. That is, certain dealers will get together and decide not to bid against each other, letting one dealer buy the object at whatever the sale price is. Afterward, a private auction is held in the hotel room and the dealers then share the money paid by the top bidder at the second and unethical auction. The seller, of course, receives the lower price from the public auction.

In other words, the buyer has to be aware of the art market just as he has to in the stock market. But there is expert advice available: there are professional art consultants, there are museum staff who will always, for a fee, gladly add their opinion on authentication.

As an investment, art has a real role to play: there is a valid market on which it can be traded and there are profits to be made, but you have to use the same prudence and rely on the same kind of expert analysis as you would in other investments.

15

About the art
of buying art

A painting by Paul Gauguin brought $950,000 in New York not long ago. It was bought by an unnamed Swiss dealer who perhaps was happy to get $50,000 change out of his $1-million cheque. The same painting sold at auction 10 years before for $275,000 — an increase of just under 350%. Not a bad investment for the man who bought it at the auction a decade earlier.

On the other hand, $275,000 invested in real estate in any one of 10 Canadian cities would likely have brought a six-fold return or even 10 — possibly $2.5 million.

The acquisition of a collection of art objects needs time, money and a great deal of expertise. It needs extra insurance and it also needs more security than most premises normally have. After all, art thefts are a fact of life nowadays, and in the last little while even major museums have been plundered by extremely competent art thieves. Saying that, however, does not detract from the real advantages that will accrue to anyone who decides to put together an art collection.

It is possible to buy art as an investment hedge against inflation, but, as the sale of the Gauguin shows, the funding has to be very large. Impressionist paintings — that is, paintings by such artists as Renoir, Van Gogh, Monet, or Manet — if they are worth buying, start at $200,000 a piece. Chinese vases, especially of the Ming period, have traded recently as high as $500,000. Any established artist of this century, such as Picasso, Miro and Matisse, are in the range of $100,000-$500,000, depending on the size and quality of the work.

Charles Armstrong and Roger Lace, for example, writing in the University of Western Ontario Business Quarterly for Autumn 1974, say that: "It would perhaps appear that Canadian fine art is a legitimate form of investment diversification. It has shown remarkable growth and has outpaced the stock market in the last 10 years."

So it has, but almost everything else has outpaced the stock market in the last 10 years too.

In any case, the kind of prices that Lace and Armstrong are talking about are no real hedge against inflation. Prices for paintings by A. Y. Jackson have fluctuated between $1,200-$2,800 in the last 10 years. Even if you had 20 A. Y. Jacksons, that is no great hedge against inflation in big-money terms.

The majority of Canadian works of art for which there is only beginning to emerge a valid market go for around $5,000 to $25,000. Over the next 10 years that might double, but, since everybody is now on the bandwagon for Canadian art, and since many of the great collections in the museums have been established and refined, the prices are hardly at take-off point.

If you are not going to involve yourself in the collection of paintings costing $250,000 each on the international market, but are going to concern yourself with the buying of Canadian art for other reasons, then we can forget about all the large claims, which are made on the slenderest of foundations.

For a collection of Canadian art there are some very simple rules to observe — rules that have been succinctly enunciated by Marianne Friedland. Friedland has degrees in economics and civil engineering; was a marketing consultant, business writer and art consultant before she made her avocation her career by opening a gallery in Toronto — the Marianne Friedland Gallery.

"The combination in art of sound investment with social motives is most attractive to businessmen, because it permits them to indulge the same attributes — creativeness, shrewdness and adventuresomeness — that make them successful in commerce. As the art increases in value, the collection reflects not only their good taste, but their sound judgment," she says as a preface.

106

What should you know and what are the pitfalls to avoid?

— Recognize that, while art can indeed be a good investment, only a tiny percentage of all art works produced have any real value. Most art is little more than decoration and most artists will always remain undiscovered. The secret to selecting art of value is quality.

Quality in art cannot be adequately defined and yet it is of the essence. It is what art is all about and what collecting is all about. Put simply, some pictures are better than other pictures and it is this truth that people often have difficulty understanding.

It is quality that in the long run determines both the aesthetic and the monetary value of a collection. There is by no means unanimous opinion on quality, but there is a consensus among the most informed scholars, historians, dealers and collectors.

— Acquire the service of a good dealer/consultant to guide you in your decisions (as you would in any other professional matter that relates to your business).

Although art often is treated as a commodity, it is unlike other commodities. To purchase art intelligently requires awareness, insight and sensitivity as well as knowledge of art history and an awareness of the art market. Consequently, the accumulating of a collection of high quality can hardly be accomplished by a group endeavor, but is best achieved by the efforts, vision and knowledge of a single individual (or two).

— Don't purchase an instant collection, and be wary of the consultant who offers you one. Good works of art are always scarce and take time to bring together. An instant collection to decorate your walls will be just that — decoration.

— Always purchase only the best or near-best examples of an artist's work. Don't purchase a painting just because it has a famous artist's name attached to it.

— Conversely, don't make a selection if one picture catches your eye. Be sold on the merits of the artist first. Even poor artists occasionally turn out an interesting picture. When selecting an artist for possible purchase, ask yourself — where does his work fit in the stream of art history? Is what he's doing important and original? Is the general body of his work significant?

— Don't look for bargains. Remember that fine art is a commodity with a real value and not likely to be sold for less than it's worth. It's true that some galleries take higher markups than others, so some shopping around is worthwhile. But be suspicious of "real bargains" and "half-price" sales. No one will sell an item that's really worth $1,000 for $500.

— Be wary of fashion in the market. Some overpromotion does take place from time to time, and even though the artist in question may have merit, the price you are paying may well be too high. There's a difference between generally recognized fame and a bandwagon boom of an artist's works.

— Finally, buy only what you are willing to be stuck with. That way, even if you occasionally guess wrong, you'll still be able to live with pictures that you have.

All of which does not mean that art, even Canadian art, is not increasing in value . . . it is. But the kind of increases common in European and American collections cannot be expected in collections of Canadian art.

There is, of course, a middle ground between the million-dollar Impressionist picture and the $500 Canadian one. A very good collection of international works of art might be accumulated with a budget, say, of $100,000 per year. Over 10 years, that would become worth at least $2 million if not a good deal more. That could be called an investment and would be just as exciting to collect as Canadian art. But if that's what you decide, walk warily and buy wisely.

16

A checklist of
promising artists

We like to think art is bought mainly for pleasure, that money is simply the reverse coin. So when we asked commercial and public galleries across Canada to name promising artists whose works still sell at reasonable prices, we asked them not to feel bound to nominate representatives of schools that "sell well." We asked them to adhere to just two criteria: painters selected should show an unusual degree of skill and originality, and their works should be available at not more than $1,000. The result was a varied collection of traditional and experimental work by 15 relative newcomers to the Canadian art scene.

At the same time, it has been said that Canadian art is currently greatly underpriced.

And our recommendations were made by some of the most influential people in the Canadian art world. So, as well as providing present pleasure, it's also possible the works of these 15 artists just could be a good future investment.

The panel that selected the artists comprised: Paul Wong, Bau-Xi Gallery, Vancouver; Karen Wilkin, Edmonton Art Gallery; Roald Nasgaard, Art Gallery of Ontario; Mira Godard, Marlborough Godard Gallery, Toronto and Montreal; Gilles Corbeil, Galeries Gilles Corbeil, Montreal; Louise Letocha, Musée d'Art Contemporain, Montreal; Karl Mackleeman, Anna Leonowens Gallery, Halifax; Mary Sparling, Mount St. Vincent

University Art Gallery, Halifax; Ian Muncaster, Zwicker's Gallery, Halifax.

The artists selected:

Reynald Connolly; born in Montreal, his present home, in 1944. Though completely self-taught, he has devoted himself entirely to painting and graphics since 1960. Selected major exhibitions: Galerie Gilles Corbeil and Musée d'Art Contemporain, Montreal. Collections: National Gallery of Canada; CIL; Musée des Beaux-Arts, Montreal. Connolly uses collage, ink and oil on canvas. His clever manipulation of space, depth and color produces graphics of fantasy and humor. His dreamlike imagery is reminiscent of Dali, Delvaux and Magritte, his precise geometrics of Miró or Arp.

Mimi Matte; born in Regina in 1930, now living in Toronto. Has BFA from McGill University. Awards include Ontario Society of Artists' Award (1974), first prize Aviva Art Auction, Toronto (1975). Group show: New Talent, Marlborough Godard, Montreal. First one-woman show was at Marlborough Godard, Toronto, this fall. Matte makes a personal statement about peoples' emotions in a way that is sometimes hilarious, often surreal, always compelling. She has good command of her materials — acrylics, collage and glazes — and a fine sense of composition and design.

Paul Chui; born in Hong Kong in 1933, now living in Vancouver. Had his first North American show at Bau-Xi Gallery, Vancouver, last August. Chui has long been interested in the relative fleetingness of life in contrast to the enduring world. Backgrounds of ancient things — the patina on bronze, the bark of a tree, weathered boards — stand on their own as abstract paintings. The introduction of living creatures inspires reflection on the rhythm of nature and the relationship between creature and background.

Julia Schmitt Healy; born in Chicago in 1947, now living in Halifax. Graduated BFA and MFA from School of the Art Institute in Chicago. Subsequently taught there and at Dartmouth Continuing Education School, Nova Scotia. Group shows in

110

Moncton, Halifax, Hamilton and Chicago. First one-woman show at Dalhousie Art Gallery, N.S., in 1976. Collections: Art Bank; Nova Scotia Art Bank; private collections in U.S. and Canada. Though influenced by the Chicago imagist school, Healy's work has evolved into a more personal statement of life experiences, travel, street people, family and political happenings.

Danny Blyth; born in Hong Kong in 1946, now living in Halifax. Has MFA from Nova Scotia College of Art and Design. Group shows at University of Western Ontario and Columbus College, Ohio. One-man shows at Mezzanine Gallery, Nova Scotia College of Art and Design. Blyth's work is related to American color field painting with an added sense of calligraphy and an oriental reference in his work's gestural quality.

Micheline Gingras; born in Quebec, now lives in New York. Studied painting at l'Ecole des Beaux-Arts, Montreal, and photography in New York. Group shows at Sherbrooke University; Maison des Arts, Chicoutimi; Musée du Québec; private galleries; United Nations Building in New York; Ibiza and Barcelona, Spain. One-woman shows at Infinity Gallery, New York; Musée du Québec; Musée d'Art Contemporain, Montreal; Maison des Arts, Montreal; Canadian Cultural Centre, Paris. In permanent collections: Art Bank; Gallery Lerner-Heller, New York; Musée du Québec. Received Canada Council grant. Design and color, strange perspectives, a photo-realistic attention to detail and the extraordinary juxtaposition of seemingly ordinary elements all tend to create a nightmarish atmosphere, especially in her Mechanical Hand series.

Graham Peacock; born in England in 1945, now living in Edmonton. Studied at London University Goldsmith's School of Art, Leeds College of Art and the British School in Rome. Taught at Newport College of Art; now teaches at University of Alberta. Numerous one-man and group shows at the Lefebvre Gallery, Edmonton; Edmonton Art Gallery; Art Gallery of Ontario; Saidye Bronfman Centre, Montreal; Memorial University, St. John's, Newfoundland; Leeds City Gallery. Has won various awards and is represented in many public collections including the Art Bank; the Hill Trust Fund Collection, Calgary; Leeds Education Authority; Newport Art Gallery; British Embassy, Rome. His interest has always been in the relationships of colors.

Recent work juxtaposes masses of color and texture, each influencing the other.

Nicolas Tyszka; born in 1949. Lives in Edmonton. Studied at Alberta College of Art and Nova Scotia College of Art. Has exhibited at ACA Gallery, Calgary; Edmonton Art Gallery; Saidye Bronfman Centre, Montreal; Art Gallery of Hamilton. Is represented in private collections and in the Alberta Art Foundation. Recent works show a strong abstract expressionist influence and definite transition from richly inflected, near-monochrome surfaces to bolder gestural paintings incorporating areas of contrasting color.

Jan Serr; born in Dayton, Ohio, in 1943, now living in Toronto. Has MFA from University of Wisconsin. Taught there and at Sheridan College of Applied Art and Technology. Major group shows at Editions I, Ontario Arts Council; New Talent, Marlborough Godard Gallery, Montreal. In permanent collections at Hart House, University of Wisconsin, Stanley Glen Manufacturing Company, Milwaukee, and Art Bank. First one-woman show at Marlborough Godard Gallery, Montreal, 1976. Influenced by Oriental painters of the past and fascinated by the way atmosphere modifies landscape and vision modifies image, Serr paints in a style of atmospheric realism.

Christopher Gorey; born in Massachusetts, now lives in Ingonish, Nova Scotia. Studied at Boston College of Fine Art, then taught high school before moving to Cape Breton. His work, mainly in watercolors and egg tempera, reflects a deep feeling for light and texture. Landscapes and buildings are favorite subjects.

Carole Thompson; born in Vancouver in 1945, now living at Williams Lake, B.C. Graduated from Vancouver School of Art. Has exhibited in numerous group and one-woman shows at Bau-Xi Gallery, Vancouver; Burnaby Art Gallery; Vancouver Art Gallery; Victoria Art Gallery. Is represented in various private collections. Thompson's strong, lyrical translations of the land forms around her are a fine contribution to the lore of west coast painters. Her works, shaped to the contours of the land, are in vibrant acrylics on canvas.

Charlotte Hammond; born in Montreal in 1941, now lives on Nova Scotia's eastern shore. First studied under artist Eric Goldberg, then at Indiana University and the Artists' Workshop in Toronto. Her deep attachment to and involvement with the Nova Scotia landscape is reflected in her current works.

Ric Evans; lives in Toronto where he was born in 1946. Studied painting at Ontario College of Art. Taught at Three Schools of Art; now teaching at University of Toronto. Group shows at Hart House Gallery, Toronto; A Space, Toronto; Art Gallery of Ontario. Grants from Canada Council and Ontario Arts Council. Sympathetic to much minimal and process art and an intensely committed painter, Evans' rich and satisfying work has evolved from earlier stained color-field watercolors into highly systemic, geometric oils. Present works are lyrical bands of color six inches wide, arranged in vertical rows six feet in height, using oil paint on a ground of latex house paint, and executed in a serial to produce a massive parallelogram.

Lucio De Heusch; born at Sherbrooke, Quebec, in 1946, now living in Montreal. Studied engraving at Montreal School of Fine Art and University of Quebec in Montreal. Has had one-man shows at Salle des Gouverneurs, Sorel; Galerie de l'Etable du Musée des Beaux-Arts de Montréal; Salle d'Exposition du Centre d'Art d'Orford; Musée d'Art Contemporain, Montréal; Galerie Laurent Tremblay, Montreal. Won the Concours des Créateurs du Québec in 1971. Public collections: Musée d'Art Contemporain and Musée des Beaux-Arts de Montréal; Musée du Québec, Quebec City; Université du Québec à Montréal; California College of Arts and Crafts; Art Bank. In his balanced articulation of an atmosphere with a geometric surface de Heusch has made a strong start. His works are mainly in colored ink on paper.

Jaan Poldaas; born in Sweden in 1948, now living in Toronto. Studied architecture at University of Toronto. Began painting in 1971. First one-man show at A Space Gallery, 1974. Group show at Art Gallery of Ontario, 1975. The most obviously common aspects of Poldaas' work (like that of other minimalists) are reduced means, serial format, denial of illusion and illustration. No less significant, however, is the way he uses a system to achieve autonomous color. He has created a syntactical order of decoded and consequential coloring.

17

About values in fine antiques

You *could* still go into an antique shop in this country and find a pine table or a Canadian silver spoon at a bargain price. It's conceivable — but it's not likely. The days are gone when people would stop in the summer in Napanee or some other small town in Ontario or Quebec to look for a piece of pine furniture, at about $30, to give as a wedding present.

Proof? The last thing we bought on such a trip, in the mid-1960s, was a pine washstand. It looked nice, was well cleaned, and cost $25. One of exactly the same workmanship was on sale recently at the R. G. Perkins booth of the Canadian Antique Dealers Association Fair. Price? $295.

We talked with Bob Perkins about the increase.

"It's not on everything," he said. "That settee, for example, I sold for $145 about 10 years ago. I bought it back recently, and it's now only $450.

"But small things — and really old things — are getting very costly."

He showed us a small carved madonna and child, seated and crowned in splendor. The original paint was still on most of it. It had never been repainted, or repaired. $800. A copper weathervane, a folk-art horse, found in Vermont recently was $600.

At the opposite corner of the antique fair, Breitman Antiques, of Montreal, had a diamond-point armoire at $5,000 and a much

114

smaller commode with empire-arched ends and the original hardware at $4,500.

What are the reasons for the increase?

"Well," said Betty Ramsay, immediate past president of the Canadian Antique Dealers Association, "it's not that they are out of line now. They were far too cheap before. But people know what they are looking for. They've read about it. They want it. And they are prepared to pay for it. What's more, they know it is a valuable investment."

Perkins joined in: "Absolutely. We don't care about interest rates. I'll borrow whatever money I need to buy whatever is available. I can't lose on it, so long as it is good."

That's the main thing: quality. And that is what the Canadian Antique Dealers Association is all about. Up to 1967, anyone could sell "antiques" in this country. Some were very good dealers, such people as Mrs. R. Wainman-Wood of St. Andrews, New Brunswick, Mrs. C. G. Grant of the Connoisseur's Shop in Victoria, Betty Ramsay of the China Shop in Montreal, and Bill Jackson of Toronto's Paisley Shop. Others knew little and cared less.

Centennial Year's spurring of interest in the past finally got some of them together, principally at the urging of Marian Bradshaw, the founder and editor of the Canadian Antiques Collector, a specialist journal that has a steady and devoted readership. (Marian Bradshaw is reckoned to be both the voice and the conscience of the industry.)

As finally incorporated in 1967, the association "is dedicated to safeguarding the purchaser of antiques in Canada." Every one of its members stands behind his or her expertise. Something sold as of a particular period is guaranteed to be of that period. Again, if you tire of a particular piece, the likelihood is the original seller of it will eagerly buy it back, since its value has increased while you have had it.

The 62 members of the association join in Toronto at the end of May each year and fill the St. Lawrence Hall with their best objects. Each object must pass a vetting committee which consists not only of the members themselves, but also of specialists in the different fields drawn from the curatorial and research staffs of the Royal Ontario Museum, the National Gallery, the Montreal Museum of Fine Arts, and so on.

What staggers the noncollector is both the variety and the specialization.

Take Edward E. Denby, purveyor of fine arms and armor, antique firearms and militaria. His booth had some 20 or more muskets and flintlock rifles on one side of a false fireplace and as many swords (with scabbards) on the other. There were medals (with documentation of their provenance) and a suit of armor, made by a German armorer, complete with hauberk and leather accoutrements. Beautifully chased on the shoulders and greaves, it was available for $3,000.

Denby said he deals mainly with museums, but medals, smaller knives, survey instruments and such are popular with private buyers.

Other dealers deal only with Canadiana, but there is a growing and rich market for fine furniture, china, and silver.

Only recently Sotheby's in Canada found that prices for Victoriana and some European pieces were lower here than in Europe. But not any more. At the antique dealers' last fair European dealers were in attendance. Prices in the St. Lawrence Market this year reflect that.

Bill Jackson, of the Paisley Shop, had a large George III mahogany breakfront. Of superb craftsmanship and fine detail, with only two of its original glass panes replaced, and in almost mint condition, it looks well worth the $9,500 being asked.

On a smaller scale, a pair of Worcester bulb pots, in pale green with bouquets of delicately painted flowers and trimmed with gold, each eight inches wide and 6¼ inches high, were offered in the China Shop for $1,850 the pair. As Betty Ramsay pointed out, they are not only of exquisite craftsmanship, they are also very rare.

A truly original silver piece made by Paul Starr of London in 1814 is a silver-gilt racing cup presented to Colonel Nehemia Marks of St. Stephen, New Brunswick. Colonel Marks raced horses in Halifax, his colors being yellow and blue with a yellow cap.

The trophy was won by Desdemona in 1837 and by Humbug in 1838, both horses bred by Dr. Bunting, a Saint John veterinarian. It is a magnificent piece of work, its condition also mint. At $6,000, Marjorie Wainman-Wood of Lukannon Antiques, St.

Andrews, New Brunswick, thinks she is low. But she is not pushing the price too high. She would like it to stay in Canada.

In another part of the fair was a self-portrait by Sir Joshua Reynolds; some excellent (and cheap) French military prints offered by Carol Solway of Toronto; a pair of gaming tables that would enhance any poker game (Tappitt Hen, Vancouver) at $2,950 the pair; and a very ingenious, finely crafted Davenport desk in rosewood for a lady, offered by Lorenz Antiques at $1,450.

We asked Mrs. Wainman-Wood what sort of turnover she thought might be involved in the three-day show. Neither she nor Betty Ramsay would hazard a guess. But her son said that *they* certainly did well enough out of it each year to come back annually.

"And who knows how many follow-up sales we have when we get back to St. Andrews," he said.

Many thousands of dollars' worth of stuff was already sold, little red tabs on pictures and larger red labels on pieces of furniture showed that.

But what the whole fair showed was that there is now a genuine antiques market in Canada; that the Canadian Antique Dealers Association is dedicated to making that market a reputable and honest one; that the amount of stuff coming onto the market from Canada still makes Canadiana collecting an exciting and rewarding hobby; and that you don't have to go to London or New York if you want a mahogany card table ($1,050), a Robert Sharp silver soup tureen ($10,000), a whole Coalport dinner service (plates at $35.50 each).

Nor, indeed, do you have to go to Toronto. Look for the sign of the beaver encircled by the letters CADA on any antique shop door anywhere in Canada.

All you need is the desire, preferably some expertise and lots, but *lots*, of lovely money.

18

The law and your antiques 'portfolio'

The federal Cultural Property Export & Import Act may have a bearing on your decision to invest in a collection of important fine art or cultural objects — paintings, sculptures, papers and documents or other goods of major historical, archaeological scientific or cultural significance to Canada.

The act controls the export from Canada of any item in the above classes regardless of place of origin (domestic or foreign) that:

— Is of outstanding significance in its field, and
— Is of national importance to the Canadian cultural heritage, and
— Is more than 50 years old, and
— Has been in Canada at least 35 years, and
— Is the work of a deceased artist, artisan or author, and
— Has a market value in excess of certain minimums that vary with the nature of the item.

The act provides that such goods may not be exported for disposal abroad without first being offered for sale to Canadian institutions or agencies. If within a two- to six-month period after the denial of an export permit is appealed, no such institution comes forward with a view to acquiring the item at its fair market value, it may then be exported without further constraint.

To facilitate the acquisition by approved Canadian institutions

118

of these artifacts, fine art objects, papers and so on, the act provides expanded government funding for the acquisition programs of those institutions. As a further inducement, it offers to Canadian collectors selling such items to approved institutions or agencies full exemption from capital-gains tax on the appreciated value of the item to the time of disposal.

And where the item in question is given outright to an approved institution or agency, the donor may deduct, when computing his taxable income, the full appreciated value of the item to the time it was given. This provision is similar to that applying now to gifts made to the Crown.

A review board administers the awarding of export permits where required. The board's operations and the general provisions of the act come under the ambit of the Secretary of State's office.

The law is not designed to constrain the export or import of the works of living artists. These are not on the official export-control list and may be marketed internationally. But where such items are considered by the board to be of outstanding significance in their field and to be of importance to Canada's patrimony, the tax incentives are available.

A Canadian collector selling such a work by a living artist to an approved institution or agency may be exempted from the capital-gains tax on any appreciation in value to the time of disposal. Alternatively, the donor of such a qualifying item, who gives it to an approved institution or agency, may deduct in computing his taxable income, the full appreciated value to the time of disposal.

The act also controls the importation into Canada of cultural objects illicitly exported from other countries. And Canada now accedes to the UN's Educational, Scientific & Cultural Organization's international convention to that effect.

The act, in effect, gives the government the right to invade the living rooms of the nation so that furniture, painting, sculpture, silver or jewelry may not be disposed of by its owner as he may wish. The purpose of the act is threefold:

— To keep Canadian artifacts, works of art and other parts of the national heritage in Canada.

— To set up tax incentives so that people owning such property may find it advantageous to give them to national and provincial collections, or to sell them to those institutions (with lesser tax advantage).

— To enter into international agreement so that anything exported illegally from Canada may be legally recovered, and that anything imported illegally into Canada may be legally sent back.

When the Secretary of State introduced the legislation into the House of Commons for its second reading, he pointed out that we had lost artist Paul Kane's diaries to a buyer in the United States, as well as Champlain's astrolabe, and that there is always the danger that other single but important parts of Canada's history might be sent to auctions abroad.

The only way to frustrate such sales up to then had been through an emergency purchase fund set up by the government, which had been able to keep in Canada a collection of decorative art in Quebec and a Tufts printing press in the Maritimes.

That purchase fund has also repatriated from West Germany the Speyer collection of American Indian artifacts and an 18th-century portrait by Greuze, which had originally been part of the famous collection of Sir William Van Horne.

The emergency purchase fund, however, is by its very name and nature an interim measure. Now, a statutory fund to be passed yearly by Parliament can always intervene to buy for national museums such articles as become available and cannot be purchased by the museums themselves. (Most of our museums have pitiably small purchase funds.)

Everyone in the gallery and museum field agrees with this principle. The conservation of the relatively small amount of historical material that exists in Canada is essential.

The government seems, though, to have spread its net a little wide. Having established the principle that no article that can be interpreted as a national treasure can be exported without a permit, the legislation goes on to show that such articles are those more than 50 years old, not by a living Canadian artist, and have no less a value than $500-$3,000 minimum, depending on the kind of article.

In light of the recent prices in Canada for antiques — let alone national treasures — these prices seem ridiculously low. What kind of a view do we present to the world when we start rating our national treasures from $500 up?

120

What sort of a government says that everyone who owns such an article is not permitted to sell it outside Canada, to will it outside Canada, or even to give it away outside Canada, without getting into a bureaucracy that begins with a customs officer and ends with a review board meeting in Ottawa or several other places across the country at taxpayers' expense?

As stringent as this may seem, however, it pales by the side of the provision in the legislation that says that an article of international worth (a Picasso or a Monet, for example) which has been "resident" in Canada for more than 35 years is to be equally trapped at the border.

In defending the act, a government spokesman said to a seminar at the Art Gallery of Ontario recently that he agreed the prices were too low and would have to be raised. He also said the bureaucracy would be responsive and swift to act. But we have our doubts whether any Ottawa bureaucracy can ever be either swift or indeed responsive.

The denial of a permit because the article to be sold abroad is a treasure does not mean, however, that the owner cannot sell it. All that the denial of a permit can do is to postpone its sale abroad until and unless sale at a similar price can be arranged within this country.

Much of the cumbersomeness and the indecisiveness of the legislation seems due to the fact that it is modeled on legislation similar to that in operation for years in Britain and France.

In Britain, there are huge collections — such as the Chatsworth collection, the Hatfield House collection, and maybe 50 others — that have pictures and sculptures that are immensely valuable and, in effect — though they be by Rubens or Rembrandt or Titian — are English national treasures. The sale of them out of Britain, often to pay death duties, becomes a national issue, and one can see why. But in this country, there are no such collections. It looks as if the Secretary of State has built a six-foot-high barbed-wire fence in order to keep a rabbit in.

The second major thrust of the law, after its restrictive provisions, is, however, to persuade people with national treasures to give them to the public at large. There are, therefore, tax incentives within the bill that will make it possible for a person who owns, say, a valuable painting by Paul Kane or Krieghoff to donate it to a public gallery of his choosing, and charge 100% of its value off his taxable income. Even if he sells it to the gallery at a fair price, he will not have to pay capital-gains tax.

These provisions are in keeping with the spirit of the legislation, which is to keep that which is Canadian and important not only within Canada, but also within the public domain.

The spirit of the act, therefore, is right. Its application to real national treasures is valid, but its net is too wide.

Insofar as it applies to paintings and sculptures from other countries, which have acquired a Canadian "residence" in 35 years, it may well, in fact, act as a deterrent to collectors. That is surely against the very national interest with which the Secretary of State is involved. As a method of providing purchase funds for treasures, the legislation is workable and its tax incentives seem generous.

On balance, therefore, if the bureaucratic procedures can be kept to a strict minimum, and if open license permits are fairly freely given, the legislation may yet conserve our heritage and retain the goodwill of those wealthy people who can put together collections that one day will become part of that heritage.

Only time will tell, however, if the Department of the Secretary of State will be able to walk the tightrope between encouragement and constraint, thus maintaining a balance that will keep Canadian treasures in some living rooms — and the government out.

19

How to be a winner in the auction game

Cy Wilding is the vice-president of marketing and sales for Beecham Canada Ltd. Cy Wilding is an addict. His wife, Joyce, is an addict too. So is the Wildings' eldest daughter, Jen. Their addiction, however, doesn't show up in statistics and no psychiatrist is trying to break their habit.

The Wildings are auction addicts.

They were first hooked on a wet, miserable summer afternoon in the early 1970s. It was a Saturday; the weather precluded gardening, the swimming pool was wrapped in thick mist and there were no pressing chores to be done around the house. A few days earlier some friends had suggested the Wildings attend a farm auction at Brampton, just outside Toronto. Without further thought Cy and Joyce drove to Brampton.

"I was never so cold and miserable," Joyce recalls. "But then we got interested in the people and the bidding and we were really surprised at how cheaply some of the furniture went. There was a set of slat-back chairs that sold for $6 apiece. Whoever bought them got a terrific bargain."

Cy made a few tentative bids on some furniture and was mildly relieved when he was outbid.

Today, as a result of that initial auction, the Wildings are devotees. Joyce has attended a class in antiques at her local community college and, with fellow buffs, has organized the Canadian

Antique Collectors' Association. Still very much in its infancy, the association so far has a purely local membership, but plans are already under way for regular meetings with speakers and, ultimately, for an association show.

The Wildings resist any suggestion that they are experts. But they have developed a technique of buying, based on three rules to which they adhere tenaciously:

1. Attend the preview;
2. Specialize and study your specialty;
3. Set an upper dollar limit for each item that interests you and refuse to be coaxed into a higher bid.

The Wildings have mostly applied these three principles to purchasing fine furniture, because that's the main objective of their auction-going today. But they still buy other things that interest them — china, pottery, lamps — and they point out that the rules are valid whether your interest is early Canadian pine or 19th-century silverware.

We asked the Wildings to elaborate on their three guidelines.

Attend the preview.

Almost every auctioneer sets aside a day, usually a day or two before the auction, for potential customers to look over the items to be auctioned. (Most farm auctions are staged without benefit of a preview; if you plan to bid, arrive an hour early to examine the merchandise.) Take advantage of the preview to examine every item you'll bid on. Otherwise you may later, in the heady atmosphere of the auction, find yourself bidding for an item you have seen only from a distance.

When you find something at the preview that interests you, examine it closely. Is it structurally sound? An early English desk with the veneer damaged beyond repair is no bargain.

Take a particularly close, hard look at wooden furniture. Are the legs sturdy? Do the drawers slide easily? Is the back warped? Is the back of wood or heavy cardboard? The latter indicates recent manufacture.

Are the sides of the drawers fitted to the front panel with dovetail joints? And, if so, are the joints long, skinny and uneven (an indication of an old, handcrafted piece) or short and even (machine-made and hence fairly recent)? Is the piece solid wood or veneer? A veneered piece must be in good shape or repairable.

If the piece is painted, examine the legs; the paint is probably chipped there and you'll be able to see what the wood underneath is. And if you can easily enlarge a chip with a judicious fingernail, the paint, probably applied over wax, should strip easily.

At most city auctions you can buy a catalogue listing all the items for sale. The catalogues usually cost $1 or $2 and may well prove to be the best buy of the day. The auctioneer will have examined the merchandise and his catalogue comments can help; a chair you would swear is more than 100 years old may be described in the catalogue as "1920s copy of antique."

Finally, the Wildings say, the preview gives you a chance to measure the size of items. Take a tape measure. Knowledge of size is necessary because, first, you'll want to know if that love seat will fit into your living room, and second, size is important in determining how you'll get your purchases home. A large pine armoire is not going to fit into the back seat of your compact (the Wildings drive a station wagon) and the cost of cartage may turn a bargain into a costly mistake.

Specialize and study.

Unless your tastes are incurably eclectic, you'll find that as your auction experience grows your interests tend to narrow anyway. Encourage the process by learning more about your developing specializations.

In addition to attending auctions, the Wildings browse regularly in antique stores and attend all antique trade shows. "We never bid on a piece of furniture unless we have a good idea of what a similar piece would cost in a retail store," Cy Wilding says. "It's rather obvious that an auction 'bargain' which needs restoring is no bargain if you could have bought a similar piece for a comparable price."

Unless you are a craftsman of professional competence, you should also add to the auction price a figure which will cover any repair and refinishing required. How estimate the figure? "Most small antique stores refinish furniture," Cy Wilding explains. "In the store, pick out a piece of furniture comparable in size to the one you want to bid on. The dealer will give you a rough idea of repair and refinishing costs."

(The Wildings are past masters at stripping paint and varnish but now prefer to have their major purchases refinished professionally. Once they tried a "dip-and-strip" shop — most large cities have them — but never went back; they found that the saving in stripping time was more than offset by the time required to sand smooth the grain raised by the rather crude dipping process which dunks the piece in a large vat of paint remover.)

Joyce shops around very carefully before using an auction to add to her set of Limoges dinnerware; she knows to the penny what a gravy boat or dinner plate sells for. When two large consignments of her Limoges pattern went on the auction block, she confidently outbid all other collectors, knowing she was still paying less than half the retail cost of the same pieces.

The Wildings supplement their browsing and shopping expeditions with reading. (There's a reading list at the end of this chapter.) "I suppose you can buy a chair at an auction without caring when or where it was made," Cy Wilding says. "But we find our pleasure in auctions is heightened when we can identify a piece by its likely era and even its likely locale."

It was, in fact, through reading that the Wildings discovered one of their earliest novice buys had been a spectacular bargain. They had successfully bid on a bonnet chest which they got for $85. Painstakingly they restored it. Later, when their interest in furniture had blossomed, they found an indentical twin of their chest described and illustrated in a book, Gerald Shackleton's *Furniture of Old Ontario*. There they read that their chest had been made in about 1845 by pioneer craftsmen at Kitchener — and that it was worth several times the price they had paid.

Set a limit on your bidding.

"It's difficult to over-estimate the importance of establishing a top dollar figure," Cy Wilding says. "You have an idea of what the piece would likely sell for in a retail store. Then you have to determine what it's worth to *you*. Only then are you ready to take part in the heady experience of bidding."

And it is heady. The inclination to jump your bid is so strong that you stand in danger of bidding against yourself. Imagine, for example, that you and one other bidder have bid up the price of a Boston rocker and it looks certain you'll get it for your price of

$40. Waving his gavel, the auctioneer chants, "Do I hear $45? Going once for $40, going twice, going . . ." At that moment, more than one novice has jumped his own bid to $45. Auctioneers are mostly honorable men who will tell you that your first bid of $40 is sufficient but, oh, the embarrassment.

Over and above their three cardinal rules, the Wildings offer some additional tips:

Don't let bad weather keep you home. It discourages many people and you'll find the auction blessed with fewer bidders — and hence possibly lower prices — than usual.

The more auctions you attend, the more you'll get to recognize familiar faces. Some will be amateurs like yourself and some will be professionals — dealers and proprietors of antique and nostalgia stores. Watching them bid is another way to gain experience. You can estimate that the retail price of any item knocked down to the pros will be about twice what they paid at the auction, so if you know you're after something good you can confidently outbid them.

Don't be dismayed if the auctioneer's assistant bids against you. He is simply bidding for an absent bidder who has left an "advance bid" with the auctioneer. Sure, you've heard about shills but you're unlikely to meet them at reputable auction rooms.

You will occasionally hear talk of a "reserve bid." This is the lowest figure the owner of the article for sale will accept. If it's not reached, the item is withdrawn.

Get onto local auctioneers' mailing lists. Most city auctions are held weekly but auctioneers will often send out notices of more infrequent special sales.

Ask the auctioneer where he advertises. Most auction firms place regular notices in the want-ad sections of newspapers but take larger display ads for special sales — estate sales, art collections and so on.

Take money. You'll be required to pay for your purchase — cheques are acceptable — before you leave the auction room. (Auctioneers' commissions have increased recently, incidentally; 20%-25% of what you pay will go to commission.)

And unless you have lots of money, don't choose to specialize in early Canadian pine furniture. "The passion for pine has priced most pieces right out of reach," Cy Wilding says. "There are very few pieces left that haven't already been sold at auctions. When one is found, the dealers snap it up."

Because they live in Toronto, Cy and Joyce Wilding haunt the city auctions. Their three rules of auction buying, though, apply equally well to farm sales and, when they can, Cy and Joyce also go to farm auctions. "It's a social event," Cy says. "Neighbor meets neighbor. Local gossip is exchanged. It's fun for the whole family. We make a picnic out of it. Take some blankets to sit on, pack some sandwiches. It's terrific."

There are dozens of books available to help along your self-eduction as an auction-goer, some excellent, some passable, some worthless. The list below, which is divided into books of general interest and those that treat specialized areas, covers only reliable guides — well researched, convincingly authenticated works.

General
Abrahamason, Una: *Domestic Life in 19th Century Canada:* Burns & MacEachern, Toronto, 1966.
Adamson, Anthony and Marian McRae: *The Ancestral Roof: Domestic Architecture of Upper Canada:* Clarke Irwin, Toronto, 1963.
McClinton, Katherine Morrison: *Art Deco: A Guide for Collectors:* Potter, New York, 1972.
Minhinnick, Jeanne, illustrated by John Richmond: *At Home in Upper Canada:* Clarke Irwin, Toronto, 1970.

Books
Hood, Dora: *The Side Door: 26 Years in My Book Room:* Ryerson Press, Toronto, 1958.

Clocks
Burrows, G. Edmond: *Canadian Clocks and Clockmakers:* G. Edmond Burrows, Oshawa, 1973.

Glassware

Klamkin, Marian: *Depression Glass: A Collector's Guide:* Hawthorne Books, New York, 1973.

Stevens, Gerald: *Early Canadian Glass:* Ryerson Press, Toronto, 1961.

Handicrafts

Green, H. Gordon, ed: *A Heritage of Canadian Handicrafts:* McClelland & Stewart, Toronto, 1967.

Lamps

Russell, Loris S.: *A Heritage of Light, Lamps and Lighting in the Early Canadian Home:* University of Toronto Press, 1968.

Pottery

Webster, Donald: *Early Canadian Pottery:* McClelland & Stewart, Toronto, 1971.

Periodicals

Canadian Antiques Collector: Denmount Publishing Co., 200 St. Clair Ave. W., Toronto.

Ontario Showcase: The Magazine for Antique Collectors: PO Box 670, Ridgetown, Ontario.

20

Some views on gold as a long-term refuge

It has been looking for some years now as if gold has become one of those tests, like the issue of whether man is innately good or evil, that divide much of the human race into fiercely contending camps.

Liberals like John Maynard ("barbarous relic") Keynes and the U.S. Treasury Department have consistently derided gold and attempted to eliminate its monetary function. Conservatives, especially American conservatives to whom the advent of Roosevelt was a major ideological event, have tended to be friendlier. It's no accident that such hardened advocates of investing in gold as Harry Schultz advertise their services heavily in National Review —a staunch conservative voice edited by William F. Buckley Jr.

Investors should watch this, because it explains the surprising fervor that gold can evoke, not least in the financial press. The division is ultimately related to the liberal affection for reason — and what could be more tidy and rational than an SDR? — as opposed to the conservative tendency to assume various dark and occasionally unpleasant atavisms in the human mind that cannot be altered.

The conservative advocates of gold believe that the metal is still the ultimate store and standard of value. On the other hand, the weight of academic opinion has been against gold, and that has been reflected to a large extent in the press. So, in the name of balance, we'd like the reader to meet James Dines and Nicholas L. Deak — two knowledgeable men who, despite widespread disappointment in the metal's price, hold strong views on gold as a long-term refuge.

Dines' ascetic face, with its hollow cheeks and high forehead, looks disturbingly like a skull, or an 18th-century death mask. But behind fine-rimmed glasses, his cold brown eyes are unwaveringly alert. His courteous manner combines unobtrusive reduction of stock-market problems to simple terms suitable for visiting journalists with the relentless insistence upon his own prescience common to all investment-letter writers.

The Dines Letter ($150 a year; 18 East 41st Street, New York 10017) is the best known of the services produced by Dines and his small army of staff, although these services include two regular chart books, featuring point and figure charts (one-point and three-and-five-point respectively), and some money management. ("Our smallest accounts are about $100,000.") Some 5% of Dines' subscriptions comes from Canada.

This can't have been an easy period for Dines. He carried his famous partiality for gold to the point of predicting $300-$400 per ounce, once its purchase became legal in the U.S., in contrast to the short-term caution of fellow gold bugs such as Harry Schultz. His subsequent cancellation of a planned conference on gold in Carnegie Hall was hailed gleefully by the equally fanatical anti-gold forces. (But with two such conferences in the preceding months the demand might well have been sated.) Dines now says that his circulation is still within 100 of its high, although he admits, with one of his rare smiles, that his public relations director is "taking a holiday."

Unlike some of his letter-writing colleagues, Dines obviously does much of his own original technical research. He says he uses $10,000 worth of investment services every year, compiling them into a composite negative-opinion index. Fundamental research is imported.

Dines attributes his arrival at highly pessimistic hard-money conclusions to his missing the Keynesian brain-washing of contemporary economics courses. He's a lawyer, but never practised, becoming a securities analyst after two years in military intelligence.

Now in his 40s, Dines has published his letter since the early 1960s, and regards the periodic vacillations in popular enthusiasm for gold with a certain bitter contempt. He seems convinced that "the pack of crooks" making up "the Washington economic establishment" will inevitably lead the nation into socialism and total financial collapse. "I've told them the truth, and now I'm going fishing."

Dines' basic thesis is common. Government deficit spending is debauching the currency, and will eventually cause total collapse, during which gold will be the only refuge. He dislikes being asked about short-term swings, apparently regarding them as frivolous. At the moment, however, he's guarded about gold bullion's *immediate* future.

Dines' attitude to the stock market is highly critical. He places great emphasis on the deterioration in the broad range of stocks not represented in the Dow-Jones industrial average — "the invisible crash", which is also the title of his latest collection of articles, *The Invisible Crash* (Random House).

What about investors with losses on gold stocks?

"That only applies to those who bought late. They should switch, and take a tax loss, or hold. But not sell."

Although people who prophesied disaster and preached salvation in gold have seen gold prices melt away, Nicholas Deak still has a kind word for the metal. "Gold is a good investment for those who wish to sit on it for years waiting for a world monetary collapse," the president of Deak & Co. says, and that New York-based firm is the largest foreign-exchange house in the Western Hemisphere. (It has 50 offices worldwide.)

Deak sees collapse coming inevitably from the constant inflationary trend and governmental deficit spending. With the intensity of these trends varying from country to country, the faith in different currencies hasn't been affected uniformly, and a system of floating rates has had to be devised during the past few years.

Deak is concerned about the outlook for the Canadian dollar. "We have found in the past," he says, "that when a country introduces restrictions such as wage and price controls or threatens nationalizations, faith in the economy is weakened and capital outflows follow. I expect that the C$ rate will deteriorate."

By contrast, the US$ looked very good. The mark had

strength, but it was no longer the supermark it had been. Deficit spending will sooner or later take its toll. Only the Swiss franc was qualified as strong by Deak, because of the long-standing aversion for deficit spending by the Swiss government.

Under these circumstances, Deak thinks that a long-term investment in gold is safe. He believes the U.S. Treasury will not sell any more of its gold as long as the market price remains relatively low. "The price would have to rise to $170 for the Treasury to take a look at the market again," he says.

Buying precious metals on margin is to be avoided as an investment unless the margin is very high — such as 50% on a purchase of silver — so that there is no threat of getting a margin call. The man in the street should consider only ordinary gold coins — those selling at only a small premium above their metal content and that have no numismatic value, such as the South African Krugerrand which has a gold content of exactly one ounce.

21

On investing in
man's best friend

Dudley is a superstar, a natural ham who likes the smell of the greasepaint, the roar of the crowd. His whole attitude says: "Here I am — look at me."

Dudley is an Old English Sheepdog — not any old OES but king of the road, top of the heap, in fact top dog in Canada. If you could buy him, which you can't, his price would be astronomical. But Dudley is not a walking gold mine.

For breeder-owner Barbara Vanword of Newmarket, Ontario, Dudley is a $15,000 dream-come-true. That's what it has cost her since she started with a $400 bitch and a stud fee of $750 to pay. The first litter produced Dudley who, now four, has already started earning his keep with a stud fee of $500. His annual income, Ms. Vanword estimates, will be around $5,000. But he will still need to be housed, fed and cared for in a manner befitting a champion. Says Ms. Vanword: "You're lucky if you break even, but I feel happy to have set a goal and made it."

Shang, a charismatic Chow and Canada's number two dog, needs only one more win to set a world record for his breed. His owners, Herb and Joan Williams and Fred Peddie of Toronto, estimate operating costs for their kennel of six Chows and one puppy, plus costs of showing, were about $20,000 last year. Their income from their dogs? Shang's stud fees at $250 and the sale of maybe a couple of pups a year for $700 apiece.

Clearly Shang is not earning his kibble. But for his owners there is a different kind of joy. "The fun for us is to improve the breed," says Herb.

The dog: certainly not man's best investment. But judging from the burgeoning canine population (200,000 purebreds registered last year with the Canadian Kennel Club), and the mushrooming of dog shows and trials all across Canada, man's best friend is rapidly becoming man's favorite hobby.

There *is* money in breeding dogs, providing you go into it in a big, big way. Joyce Alden, a Dachshund breeder from Unionville, Ontario, has the biggest high-quality kennel in the country — she has 123 adults and sells 200 puppies a year — and is definitely in the black. But even she says: "You need the whole family to pitch in and help, because paying professionals is prohibitive." Her veterinary bills are $350-$500 a month and she spends about $4,000 a year on shows. Her investment in equipment alone is close to $42,000. Her gross earnings in a good year — after "more than 10 years of bone-wearying work to get the business going" — are about $25,000. And that includes boarding revenue.

For most, breeding is an expensive hobby. Editor of *Encyclopedia of Music in Canada*, Kenneth Winters breeds Pekingese. The challenge for him is in assembling bloodlines. It's a hobby he finds so absorbing that he has bought 10 acres in the country for his 30-40 dogs — meaning he has to travel about 100 miles each way daily to get to work. He spends $12,000 a year on breeding and gets back $5,000 at most.

Then there's Martin Kenney, headmaster of Balmoral Hall School in Winnipeg. He breeds Bouviers des Flandres, a comparative rarity that looks like an outsize Scottie. He is not making money. But he says: "It's the best way I can think of to keep the while family happy. Everybody participates; holidays we take together at dog shows."

Whether it's for love or money — and it had better, initially at least, be for love — how do you buy your future best friend?

All veterinarians agree on a vital first step. Buy from a reputable breeder, not a pet store. Says Dr. K. Gadd, a member of the Toronto Academy of Veterinary Science: "Buying at a pet store is extremely risky. There is a much higher incidence of sick puppies."

The problem lies not in the stores themselves but in their sources. They buy from "puppy mills," mostly in the U.S. and England, though they're appearing now in Canada too. Veterinarians say the mills' appalling production-line treatment of adult dogs and mass handling and shipping of pups is almost guaranteed to produce sickness.

Also, if you're shopping for a house pet and nothing more, you'll find breeders generally charge less than stores. (Their prices for show pups are something else.)

On to your most crucial choice — that of breed. The essential question here is: how has man treated his best friend? The answer is: not too well.

For instance, you may fancy a giant breed. Their popularity is growing fast. But the evidence indicates, in the words of one veterinarian, "most have been bred to their lethal limit." We've giant-ized them to a point where their hearts and circulatory systems can no longer support their mass. And we keep them, most unsuitably, in cities. The result is a shortened life expectancy, and an unhealthy one. Dr. Gadd says he's treating an increasing number of Great Danes for acute stress brought on by cramped living.

Lethal limits have probably been reached at the other end of the spectrum too. The extreme miniaturization of the Chihuahua is a case in point.

Almost all serious breed problems are the result of indiscriminate breeding for generations to fit certain exaggerated show standards. But for every exaggeration in a breed you pay a price — and so does the breed. The case of the Cocker Spaniel provides clear evidence. Thirty years ago, when they were fast rising in popularity and being indiscriminately bred, there were a lot of ill-tempered Spaniels grumping around. Now less popular and more selectively bred, Spaniels are again friendly pets.

Now paying the price is the Poodle, present number one dog in popularity. One breeder readily admits that Poodles have become rather neurotic. And the prevalence of hip dysplasia in our number two breed, the German Shepherd, is almost epidemic due to a show requirement of sharply sloping hindquarters.

Dysplasia, which can take up to five generations to clear from breeding stock, is also found in Labrador Retrievers, St. Bernards, Old English Sheepdogs and other large breeds.

You should also know that Pekingese and other snub-nosed breeds are prone to respiratory problems; that Dachshunds may get slipped discs; that toy breeds may get slipped kneecaps and hypoglycaemia; and that haemophilia, although rare, is present in certain strains of a dozen breeds ranging from Cairns to Collies.

Other problems and defects specific to breeds are listed at the end of this chapter.

So is *anything* safe to buy? Yes, provided you take certain precautions:

— Protect your purchase with X-rays and guarantees. A good breeder will show you certified X-rays of both parents and give you a guarantee (usually 12-month) against specified genetic defects; the guarantee should call for replacement of the dog if a defect shows up.

— For temperament defects, take a close look at the mother; that's where a pup gets most of its characteristics from.

— Buy from a breeder who willingly discusses a breed's good and bad points. Anything else is a snow job; there's scarcely a breed without a single defect or drawback.

— Have any prospective purchase checked by your own veterinarian and get him in on the writing of the guarantee.

— If you opt for a highly popular breed, choose a breeder who is, as Joyce Alden says, "substituting for what nature would have done by survival-of-the-fittest selection for breeding" — in other words, someone who's breeding for overall sound quality, not for showy externals.

— Be knowledgeable. Read up on the breeds. Attend shows and talk to breeders. (The monthly Dogs in Canada publishes show calendars and its companion publication, Dogs Annual, lists breeders and breeders' associations.)

So now you have the dog. And maybe you should stop right there; the next stage can be both costly and addictive. But if you've bought a show-quality pup and feel like going on, here's what happens at stage two, the show ring.

Some 300 shows are held every year in Canada. Serious breeders like Herb Williams attend 75 or more. Entry fees are $10-$15, handling fees $25-$75, depending on the importance of the show.

You may elect to handle your dog yourself but it's an expert task and all-important in winning; one Canadian champion has just been retired only because owner and handler fell out and a new handler couldn't possibly come in and immediately develop the degree of dog/human rapport required to show well.

Expect no immediate return from showing. Trophies and ribbons, not cash, are awarded at most dog shows. In the very few exceptions, the cash goes not to the owner but to the handler.

If your sights are already on stage three — breeding — your paragon must carry off at least one championship (based on an accumulation of points at various shows) and several group wins. A group winner is the dog that triumphs when best-of-breed winners in a show go on to compete within one of six groups, viz. working, hounds, terriers, toys, sporting, non-sporting.

Breeding should not be approached lightly; matching bloodlines is a careful and painstaking craft. It's a judicious blend of mix and match and you'll need all the help and advice you can get from a good veterinarian.

You must also have patience; a bitch shouldn't be bred until she's at least 1½, and then only once a year. Her breeding career will likely be over by the time she's seven. Size of litter you may expect parallels size of breed; a toy may have only one or two pups while a large breed may have more than 10. If you're lucky, the first litter may just pay for the mother's veterinary and stud fees.

A male is also ready for breeding at about 1½. But there's no guarantee your top dog will be in demand as a stud; when Chuk T'Sun of Caversham, a Pekingese with $60,000 in show costs behind him and a record of 126 U.S. best-in-show wins, was made available to Canadian breeders at a paltry $50, he was used only once.

All this while, of course, you're housing and feeding the apple of your eye and providing veterinary services. Breeders reckon this ranges from $1 a day for a small breed up to $2.50 a day for a giant. Capital costs can go as high as you want; ideally you should have a minimum of three acres close to a large metropolitan centre.

Even so, you say, it should be possible to make money by breeding very selectively and eschewing the expensive show circuit? Ah, but if you want to sell your dogs, you have to advertise them. And that means showing.

138

There's no easy answer. But then the dedicated breeders aren't looking for easy answers. To be a breeder of skill requires that you be, as Kenneth Winters says, "a combination of artist, scientist and geneticist." The challenge is to improve the breed and the perfect masterpiece is always just around the corner.

Following is a wise buyer's guide to the various breeds of dogs. They're listed in order of popularity ratings, which have been based on American Kennel Club statistics. The costs given are approximate; in the pet category, the costs are for pups bought as sound household pets; in the investment category, they're for top-quality show/breeding stock.

1. **Miniature Poodle.** *As a pet:* Ideal family pet, intelligent, independent, affectionate. Non-shedding coat doesn't cause allergies but needs trimming. Cost, $100 and up. *As an investment:* Forget breeding; too many in it already. Though Canada has excellent poodles, best stock still comes from England. Cost, at least $1,500 for a good one; stud fee $100 and up. *Genetic problems:* Slipped kneecaps in toy size; not visible till four to six months but renders affected leg useless by 10-12 months. Also retinal atrophy leading to blindness.

2. **German Shepherd.** *As a pet:* Most easily trained dog. Usually attached to one or two people; not recommended as family pet because of its over-protectiveness. Close coat needs little care except brushing. Needs considerable exercise. Cost, $200 and up. *As an investment:* Popularity ensures demand for pups. Not many goods ones in Canada. Best stock still comes from Germany. Cost, $16,000 and up. Stud fee $200. *Genetic problems:* Breeding for extreme hip' angulation favored by judges has caused bone abnormalities; main defect is hip dysplasia, also shoulder problems.

3. **Irish Setter.** *As a pet:* Beautiful but hard to train. Sheds hair. Needs much exercise, brushing and discipline. Cost, $200 and up. *As an investment:* Popular in the show ring. Good pups should sell well. Cost, at least $350; stud fee $100 and up. *Genetic problems:* Hip dysplasia and progressive retinal atrophy.

4. **Beagle.** *As a pet:* Exceptionally good-natured, active and alert. Tendency to wander; its nose carries it away. Little groom-

ing needed. Cost, about $75. *As an investment:* Not much money in breeding; few entered in show ring. Cost, $250-$350; stud fee minimal. *Genetic problems:* None.

5. **Dachshund.** *As a pet:* Six breeds available; standard and miniature versions respectively of the smoothhair, longhair and wirehair. Good family pet; friendly, not aggressive. Gluttony is its only notable vice. Cost, $125 and up for standard, $175 for miniature. *As an investment:* Can be profitable to breed, particularly longhaired and wirehaired which are on the upswing. Cost, $300-$500; stud fee $150. *Genetic problems:* Bad backs and slipped discs. Smoothhairs may have skin problems.

6. **Doberman Pinscher.** *As a pet:* One of the most intelligent and easily trained breeds, also one of the most maligned. Very protective but also very good-natured in home surroundings. Needs plenty of exercise but little grooming. Ears and tail usually cropped. Cost, $200 and up. *As an investment:* A possibility; the field is crowded but there's a demand. Cost, $350 and up; stud fee $150 and up. *Genetic problems:* Rare cases of hip dysplasia. Uncertain temperament.

7. **Miniature Schnauzer.** *As a pet:* Friendly, perky; a good city dog. Has great appeal for man who doesn't want to be seen walking a powder-puff. Needs hand stripping (thinning) or clipping. Cost, $200 and up. *As an investment:* Good; the breed is upcoming and hasn't yet been spoiled. Cost, $500 and up; stud fee $100 and up. *Genetic problems:* Micropthalmia creates a disposition to cataracts. Skin problems resulting from rough coat.

8. **Labrador Retriever.** *As a pet:* Strong, active, good-natured; good family dog though a bit boisterous for very small children. Loves outdoors. Needs little grooming. Cost, $150 and up. *As an investment:* Easy to breed. Many good ones available in Canada; breed has not been spoiled. Cost, $350 and up; stud fee $100 and up. *Genetic problems:* Hip dysplasia.

9. **American Cocker Spaniel.** *As a pet:* Once practically ruined from overbreeding, but now much improved. Excellent temperament, needs grooming. Cost, $150 and up. *As an investment:* Good. Cost, $350 and up; stud fee $100. *Genetic problems:* Eyes (cataracts), ears (prone to infections).

10. **St. Bernard.** *As a pet:* Needs daily walks, lots of space and a cool climate. Massive size to which it has been bred shortens life

140

expectancy and often produces genetic weakness. Has very gentle disposition but makes a good pet only in the right (spacious) environment. Buy only the best. Cost, $250-$300. *As an investment:* Keep away. Has been badly overbred. Cost of rearing pup is phenomenal. Also care must be taken in exercising; bones are soft up to three years. Cost, $300 and up; stud fee $250. *Genetic problems:* Veterinarians report nine out of 10 have hip dysplasia. Also prone to twisted-leg syndrome, dry shoulder sockets, in-turning and out-turning eyelids.

11. **Rough Collie.** *As a pet:* Good disposition. Long shedding coat needs much combing: also needs running room, and feels the heat. Good collies being bred in Canada, especially in the west, and breed has not been spoiled. Cost, $200. *As an investment:* Fair; breeding the fine head is difficult. Not much demand. Cost, up to $5,000 for a really good one; stud fee $200. A better investment would be the Shetland Sheepdog; it's smaller and becoming popular. *Genetic problems:* Collie-eye syndrome (similar to progressive retinal atrophy), also dysplasia and weak rear end.

12. **Pekingese.** *As a pet:* Ideal for apartment and city life; good watchdog, personality-plus, good temperament. Requires cool temperature and lots of brushing. Cost, $250 and up. *An investment:* Not recommended; bitches are not good whelpers, often requiring Caesarian births. Cost, $400-$700; stud fee $100-$150. *Genetic problems:* Subject to skin irritation between the eyes. Eyes prone to injury because they protrude. Respiratory problems.

The following breeds are considered to be "comers."

Lhasa Apso. *As a pet:* Has terrier temperament; inherently wary of strangers but essentially gentle. Needs much combing. Enjoys home life and daily walk. Cost, $250 and up. *As an investment:* Good bet; getting very popular. Cost, $650 and up; stud fee $200. *Genetic problems:* Prone to slipped kneecaps.

Shih Tzu. *As a pet:* Popular as a house pet because of its good-natured, humorous personality. Needs some exercise and much brushing of its long, dense coat. Cost, $175 and up. *As an investment:* Good bet; like Lhasa Apso, getting very popular. Cost $350-$400; stud fee $250. *Genetic problems:* Prone to slipped kneecaps; protruding eyes may cause problems.

Bichon Frise. *As a pet:* Good-natured, gentle, intelligent, with the daintiness and neatness of a poodle. Just introduced to Canada, could be comer of all breeds. Perfect size for city living. Cost, $350. *As an investment:* Very good bet. Field is wide open and the breed promises to become big in North America. Cost, $400 and up; stud fee $350. *Genetic problems:* None so far.

22

How tax indexing helps and why it hurts, too

Don't count too heavily on that welcome annual relief provided by income-tax indexing. It could hasten the day of tax-rate increases, to make up for government revenue lost through indexing.

Although rising prices bite into your savings, they're also helping to moderate automatic tax increases biting into your income. Improbable as that may sound, the tax indexing system — started in taxation year 1974 and pegged to the consumer price index — has begun to provide significant relief from tax on income gains that are directly related to inflation.

The basic personal exemptions applicable in 1973 ($1,600 standard exemption, for instance) and the basic tax brackets (say $14,000-$24,000) were increased by 30.7% for the 1976 taxation year. That compares with a 17.4% increase in those basic amounts in 1975 and a 6.6% increase in 1974.

In 1974, the government estimated that one year's increase in the indexing factor would reduce federal government coffers by more than $750 million in tax year 1975. It was estimated to cost more than $1 billion in 1976. This raises the possibility of tax increases.

There are those who recommend increases to help cool inflation, and those who don't. But no one doubts that indexing is gradually adding more pressure for tax increases — or, presumably, for

143

some form of adjustment to the indexing formula itself.

A 30.7% indexing factor pushes the standard personal exemption available to everyone up to $2,091 from $1,878 in 1975, $1,706 in 1974 and $1,600 in 1973.

A married man, whose wife has no income of her own, and with two young children, could reduce taxable income by $4,705 vs $4,226 in 1975 and $3,600 before indexing started. For a single pensioner, the age exemption of $1,307 plus the $2,091 basic exemption provides a total reduction of taxable income equal to $3,398, vs $3,052 in 1975 and $2,600 in 1973.

The lowest tax bracket is defined at $654, vs $587 in 1975. The top bracket — where the highest marginal rate takes effect — would rise to $78,420 from $70,440 in 1975 and $60,000 in 1973. This means, of course, that it takes a higher income to push the individual taxpayer into a higher tax bracket.

The investor with a high proportion of income from ordinary dividends is particularly fortunate — and this advantage will grow as the indexing factor increases. Although dividends are increased (or "grossed-up") by one third to arrive at taxable income, the impact of the increase is softened by indexing. Yet the dividend tax credit (slightly higher than the gross-up and which reduces tax payable) isn't affected.

Clearly it doesn't make any difference for individuals with less than $1,000 of interest and/or grossed-up dividend income. They don't pay any tax on this income. But for those with a larger investment income, and for retired individuals, dividends could look ever more attractive from a tax point of view.

Take a retired pensioner with $15,000 of income — half of it from ordinary dividends, the other half in the form of pension and interest income. With an indexing factor of 30.7% in 1976, tax is about 54% less than would be the case without indexing. Had all the income been from interest and pension, the reduction from indexing would have been only about 16%.

This example assumes the pensioner is single, claims the indexed personal exemptions totaling $3,398 and non-indexed deductions of $1,000 for a pension (other than Old Age Pension, Canada or Quebec Pension Plans), the $1,000 interest/dividend deduction, and $100 automatic reduction for charitable contributions. It also assumes provincial tax equal to 30.5% of federal tax.

The inflation factor for each tax year is the ratio of the average "adjusted" consumer price index for the 12-month period ending Sept. 30 immediately before the year in question to the average price index for the 12-month period ending Sept. 30, 1972. Thus, the factor for 1976 is the ratio of the average consumer price index for the 12 months ending Sept. 30, 1975, to the average for the 12 months ended Sept. 30, 1972.

The term "adjusted consumer price index" means the index for that period as adjusted in the manner prescribed by regulation. The idea was to provide flexibility to adapt if, say, there were changes made in the method of weighting the price index or if certain aberrations made the results unreasonable. Presumably this flexibility could be used to adjust the tax indexing factor for a number of reasons. So far, the actual consumer price index has been used.

According to the rules of the system, the tax indexing factor will rise each year as long as prices advance. It won't decline in any case — even in the unlikely event that prices decline from one year to another. The legislation specifically states that the tax indexing factor won't be adjusted downward.

Although introduced by the federal government, indexing automatically affects provincial tax in all provinces except Quebec. That's because provincial tax (which varies from province to province) is calculated as a percentage of federal tax. Quebec, which collects its own income tax, hasn't introduced a companion indexing plan, opting instead for personal tax changes designed to ease the effects of inflation.

Although indexing has been in effect for some time, it still isn't fully understood. The idea is to eliminate the progressive element of tax increases that occur simply as a result of inflation. In any non-indexed progressive tax system, as income rises, tax rises at a faster rate. This happens even when the purchasing power of the bigger income doesn't increase.

Without indexing, governments tend to have a vested interest in inflation, since their revenues automatically increase as prices rise.

But it's important to emphasize that the introduction of indexing doesn't mean that taxes won't rise.

As pointed out, the mounting revenue cost suggests that some governments may move to make up the difference through increases in personal or other taxes.

One of the strong arguments in favor of indexing is that if governments want more revenue, they must achieve this through highly visible tax increases rather than through invisible, inflation-induced increases.

Indexing doesn't remove all the tax on income gains due to inflation. It won't mean, for instance, that if income rises by an amount equal to the indexing factor, tax will be the same as if there'd been no increase in income and no indexing.

In theory, the system works this way: if the individual's income gains merely keep pace with inflation, his *real* after-tax income will be about the same as if he had no increase in income and there was no inflation. The government, in turn, gets about as much revenue, in *real* terms, as it would if there were no increase in income and no inflation.

Canada's indexing system doesn't, in fact, work strictly according to theory. It's distorted in a number of ways — by the $200 minimum and $500 maximum feature of the 8% federal tax reduction, for instance. Then, too, only personal exemptions are indexed. The limits on other allowable deductions — such as contributions to pensions and RRSPs, the $1,000 pension deduction and the $1,000 interest/dividend deduction, charitable donations, working expenses, child-care deduction and so forth — are *not* indexed.

Capital gains aren't indexed either. This is a contentious issue since some, if not most, of the increase in capital is frequently induced by inflation rather than an increase in real value.

Since its introduction, the pros and cons of tax indexing have been debated — practicality, equity, effect on government revenues and economic implications. It remains to be seen if and when it will be extended. But at least some observers of the economic scene urge caution until the whole subject of indexing (of transfer payments as well as tax) are more thoroughly assessed.

23

When it makes sense
to prepay your mortgage

So you bought a house for $80,000, paying down $20,000, and securing $60,000 in mortgages at 12% amortized over 25 years. At the end of that time, you'll have paid $125,742 in interest or a total of $205,742 for your house.

Should you repay your mortgage at a faster rate in order to save some of that seemingly excessive interest charge? Put another way, should you invest in your own mortgage? That's a question that perplexes Canada's four million mortgage borrowers.

On a straight dollar calculation, investing in your own mortgage can save you a significant amount in interest payments.

Consider a $25,000 mortgage at 9% over 25 years. Your monthly payment would be $207. If you paid in an additional $20 per month, the net reduction on your mortgage would be $10,556. If you paid an extra $1,000 per year you would save $21,511. (See the chart on page 149 and the table on page 153.)

The reason you achieve these savings is because extra payments reduce the period over which the mortgage is amortized. For example, the $25,000 mortgage at 9% would normally be paid off in 25 years. By paying an extra $1,000 per year, the amortization period is reduced to 12 years. In other words you'll have paid off your total mortgage in 12 years, thus saving yourself the stream of interest payments from the 13th year to the 25th year.

The principle of saving large sums by contracting the amortization period holds true even if you were to go into the market-place and borrow short term at higher rates of interest. So, taking our example of a 9%, $25,000 mortgage, if you were to borrow $1,000 annually at the going rate of interest, say, 13½%, repay it over each year, and use it to prepay your mortgage, you'd still end up saving $20,690. In this situation you'd repay each year the $1,000 borrowed — at $89.56 per month — in addition to making your mortgage payments of $207. (The table on page 154 gives another example.)

"People find this difficult to comprehend because the decision to make investment choices is usually governed by the simple arithmetical comparison of interest rates," argues Robert Yeaman, manager of Finance Services Ltd. — a computer service bureau that provides mortgage analysis for homeowners. "But in this situation the saving results from the contraction of the amortization period," Yeaman points out.

However, the seemingly beneficial aspect of prepaying your mortgage is complicated by the fact that you're paying in money at the beginning of your mortgage term to get money at the end. This creates two series of cash flows. The first represents your additional investment of $1,000 per year for the first 12 years, the second represents the benefits created by the interest avoidance, starting (in our example) from the 12th year.

How do you compare a stream of future benefits against a flow of current payments? One way is to bring both to present values. Using a set of annuity tables and discounting the stream of payments avoided between year 12 and year 25 at 8% (8% is the discount rate arbitrarily selected to reflect the rate of inflation and the risk of waiting to secure the benefit), the present value of your future benefit is $7,776. Or, put another way, receiving $7,776 today is equivalent to receiving at the end of 12 years $21,511 paid in monthly installments over a 13-year period.

Using the same principle and the same rate of discount, the cost of your investment of $1,000 per year for 11 years is $7,138. The ratio between the two series of cash flows is the net yield on a present value basis: Net yield = (the present value of your future benefit) divided by (the present value of your current payments). In this example it's 1.09%.

So the net yield on a present value basis is equivalent to the

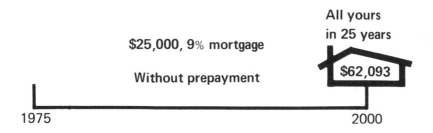

$25,000, 9% mortgage

Without prepayment

All yours in 25 years

$62,093

1975 — 2000

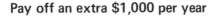

Pay off an extra $1,000 per year

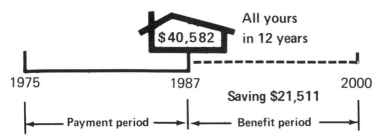

All yours in 12 years

$40,582

1975 — 1987 — 2000

Saving $21,511

|← Payment period →|← Benefit period →|

mortgage rate minus the discount rate, which is your estimation of future uncertainty over inflation et al. So if, in our example, we'd selected a 5% discount rate, the net yield would have been roughly 4%.

But most long-term investments should be measured against some kind of discount rate too. So, to analyze how investing in your own mortgage stacks up against alternative investments, it may be better to compare future benefits.

As an example we assume that Mr. Jones and Mr. Smith each invest $1,000 per year for 12 years.

Mr. Jones puts his investment in his 9%, $25,000 mortgage, paying it off in 12 years. He then puts the money he has avoided paying on his mortgage into an investment that pays him an after-tax yield of 10%. At the end of 25 years he will have accumulated $67,628.

Mr. Smith, meanwhile, puts his $1,000 per year for the first 12 years in an investment that pays him an after-tax yield of 10%. If he stops that investment after 12 years and allows the interest on his investment to compound, his accumulated investment at the end of 25 years will be $70,308. So Mr. Smith will earn $2,680 more than Mr. Jones.

However, if Mr. Smith's pre-tax yield is 10%, but after the payment of taxes his yield is 7%, then the amount he'll accumulate in 25 years will be $42,817. Since Mr. Jones doesn't pay taxes on the benefit he receives from investing in his own mortgage, his total gain in 25 years will be greater than Mr. Smith's.

But there's a further complication — the $1,000 tax credit on interest or dividend income. With that benefit, Mr. Smith would begin paying tax on his investment in the seventh year. However, if Mr. Jones takes the cash flow he receives from the 12th year onwards, and invests it, he wouldn't begin paying taxes until the 15th year. This leaves him in a better situation relative to Mr. Smith.

From this follow certain conclusions:

— That the maximum you can earn from investing in your mortgage is the rate of your mortgage. Thus, you'll never be able to do better than 11% on an 11% mortgage.

— If an alternative investment gives you an *after-tax* return that's greater than your mortgage rate, then it's not advisable to invest in your mortgage.

— Conversely, if your mortgage rate is greater than the after-tax rate that you can get on normal investments, then you might consider investing in your own mortgage.

So somebody with a marginal tax rate of 50% (a resident of British Columbia or Ontario, for instance, with taxable income of around $28,000) who decides to prepay $1,000 each year on a 9% mortgage would have to earn 13.4% on, say, his preferred or common dividends to obtain an equivalent future benefit.

Following are some *disadvantages* of investing in your own mortgage:

1. You don't receive the benefits for a number of years, at which time the benefit received is equivalent to the payments you would have made in those years.

2. The benefit is inflexible because it's limited by a certain maximum rate of return. You can't occasionally update your investment to take advantage of higher interest rates. For instance, if, 10 years ago, you'd started paying off your 7% mortgage, then

the maximum benefit you'd be receiving today would be 7%.

As Nicholas Davy, a Toronto financial analyst who has made a special study of these situations, says: "When you lock yourself into paying off a mortgage, you have a very definitive, deterministic calculation. There's nothing you can do about it. You'll get whatever the mortgage rate is, minus the rate of inflation, but you'll never get more than the mortgage rate."

3. Since Canadians move, on average, every five years, there's not much to be derived in terms of interest avoidance for the typical houseowner investing in his own mortgage.

4. If you intend to move within a few years of purchasing your home, a large open first mortgage can sometimes facilitate a sale. Prepaying could weaken this advantage.

5. Unlike stocks or a bond bought at a discount, investing in your own mortgage allows no opportunity for capital gains.

6. You forego current cash flexibility, because, in terms of your mortgage contract, your installments remain fixed (only the amortization will vary).

And these are some *advantages* of prepaying your mortgage:

1. You'll secure a future rate of return (in dollar terms) equivalent to your mortgage rate.

2. It provides a secure vehicle for investing excess funds.

3. There are no commission charges or broker's fees (although with some mortgages a penalty is imposed for prepaying).

4. The benefit you derive from your investment is tax-free. So, unless you can shelter any alternative income from taxation, the net disposable funds available from that income at the end of the period could be much less.

5. You're less exposed to the risk of alternative investments, such as stocks, because you're *guaranteed* an actual dollar saving in the future.

6. Although nobody wins with inflation, technically inflation might hurt a mortgage less than it does other investments. Yeamen sums it up this way: "Since an investment accrues with time, its present worth is minimized by inflation."

7. It could offer security-minded homeowners an emotionally satisfying experience.

When is it most prudent to pay your mortgage? If the mortgage debt is relatively large. If the amortization period has a long way to run — and particularly if the mortgage rate is relatively high.

What prepayment facilities do you normally enjoy? While second mortgages are usually open, a number of first mortgages stipulate that the borrower just can't automatically increase his payments each month. However, some first mortgages contain anniversary prepayment privileges. Once a year, a borrower may be able to pay specified additional amounts on his mortgage.

For example, conventional first mortgages through many banks may be prepaid in the first three years. Upon request, however, you may be allowed to continue prepaying as much as 10% of the original amount of the loan.

How prepayments can reduce a mortgage

25-year mortgages amortized over 25 years:

	$25,000 @9%	$40,000 @10%	$60,000 @11%	$80,000 @12%
Monthly payment.....	$207.00	$357.80	$577.53	$825.52
Total cost of mortgage ...	$62,093.72	$107,333,32	$173,239.77	$247,654.95

If payment of an extra $20 a month is made:

Revised cost of mortgage ...	$51,537.00	$92,850.99	$154,215.16	$223,615.21
Net reduction..	$10,556.72	$14,482.33	$19,024.61	$24,039.74
Mortgage paid off in ..	19 years	20 years, 6 months	21 years, 7 months	22 years, 1 month

If an extra $1,000 is paid each year:

Revised cost of mortgage ...	$40,582.07	$74,463.27	$126,505.55	$186,133.11
Net reduction..	$21,511.65	$32,870.05	$46,734.22	$61,523.84
Mortgage paid off in ..	11 years, 11 months	14 years, 1 month	16 years, 2 months	17 years, 1 month

Source: Finance Services Ltd. division of Multiple Access Ltd.

Is it worth borrowing to prepay a mortgage?

	Mortgage: $25,000 @ 9%	Mortgage: $40,000 @ 10%
Monthly payment on 25-year mortgage	$207.00	$398.83
Total cost of mortgage	$62,093.72	$119,639.81
Monthly cost of borrowing a $1,000 prepayment each year @ 13½% and repaying it that year	$89.56	$89.56
Revised cost of mortgage (cost of borrowing prepayments included)	$41,402.89	$80,135.17
Net reduction	$20,690.83	$39,504.64
Mortgage paid off in	12 years	14 years

Source: Financial Services Ltd. division of Multiple Access Ltd.

24

Mortgages as a vehicle for personal investors

Mortgages could become a far more attractive investment for Canadians who manage their own money. As part of a package of housing incentives, the federal government has made a commitment to get a federal mortgage exchange corporation into operation. While the dusting off of this idea again raised hollow laughter among those who for a decade had seen it come and go like a mirage, a true marketplace where existing mortgages can be freely traded is an urgent necessity. Too many lenders, including individual investors, have been too cautious about committing money to mortgages because they knew they couldn't sell them readily.

To reduce the cyclicality in housing expenditure, a more stable supply of funds flowing into mortgages is required. This can be achieved, in part, by the establishment of an organized secondary mortgage market. Canada has had no formal market where mortgages can be traded, like the exchanges for stocks and bonds. There hasn't been even an over-the-counter market where bids asked could be matched with bids received. The purpose of an exchange is to improve the quality of the mortgage instrument, and that attracts more of the investor's dollar during periods of credit stringency.

Canada's housing stock in the postwar period has grown phenomenally — as have mortgage loans. But despite the present size of the market, mortgages still react more sensitively than other credit instruments to restrictive monetary policy. This results in a greater decline in the relative share of funds going into mortgages. Consequently, the growth of the mortgage market to its present size has been sporadic. Major declines in the rate of growth in residential construction occurred during 1957, 1960, 1966, and 1970. In each instance the decline began about the time monetary policy became restrictive.

Traditionally, mortgage yields have been higher than yields on non-mortgage instruments. However, in the initial period of monetary restraint the yields on these non-mortgage investments rise more rapidly than the yields on mortgages. As a result, financial flows, which are quite sensitive to alternative investment yields, are apt to find their way into other markets during the initial upward shifts in the interest rate. The typical market-adjustment process begins with short-term paper, then corporate bonds, then mortgages. Thus the yields on newly issued corporate bonds rise more quickly than the effective yields on current mortgages. Hence, the corporate borrower is able to outbid the mortgage borrower during periods of heavy loan demand and credit stringency.

The sluggishness of the mortgage rate, vs other yields, has been due mainly to the absence of a secondary mortgage market. Without this market, rates have been adjusted by financial intermediaries after changes in market conditions occurred, rather than responding readily — as do other credit markets — to the changes in yield on outstanding issues.

Another reason is that many mortgage commitments are arranged in advance of the final payments of funds. These commitments are entered into at rates of interest prevailing at the time the arrangement is made. This might be six months or a year before the monies are disbursed. The effect of this time lag between mortgage-loan commitments and actual disbursement is a stabilization of interest rate.

Furthermore, many financial institutions tend to specialize more heavily in business loans and thus feel a primary allegiance to business borrowers. Also, builders and home buyers typically have high debt/equity ratios. So in times of monetary restraint, they're deemed to be marginal risks by lenders. As a result, they may be the first to have their loan requests rationed or refused.

Other factors accounting for the sensitivity of mortgages to tight monetary policy relate to certain weaknesses inherent in the mortgage instrument. One such weakness stems from its perceived inflexibility. Prior to 1970, most mortgages were amortized over 20-25 years, and the market is still dealing with this historical deficiency. But, the *major* flaw in the mortgage instrument has been its illiquidity. Investors have been normally locked in for a number of years as there has been no centralized exchange to facilitate trading. (Unless, of course, they've been prepared to sell at huge discounts.)

Other deficiencies pertain to the acquisition and administration of a mortgage. To originate a mortgage, it's necessary to check not only the personal background and financial standing of the borrower, but also the intrinsic value of the property. This involves lawyers, appraisers, credit reports. And to service a mortgage requires far more effort than the near-automatic clipping of a coupon.

Since the nature of the mortgage instrument does much to determine the supply of mortgage credit, the residential mortgage market, despite its size, is a residual one. To improve the mortgage instrument, government had been urged to institute further legislative innovation to improve the liquidity of mortgages, correcting a major flaw in a fairly attractive instrument.

Statutory changes since the 1960s already have done much to improve the characteristics of mortgages. The introduction of the five-year renewable term in 1970 improved its flexibility considerably. Investors today, therefore, are assured of periodic shifts in interest rates consistent with changes in market rate. The advent of insurance on a number of conventional mortgages — in addition to the government-insured NHA loans — has done much to mitigate the inherent risk of capital loss. Many mortgages can now be likened to government paper and traded without particular regard to the underlying value of the property. An investor now can upgrade his yield without incurring greater risk. During inflationary periods, the quality of mortgages improves more than the quality of bonds.

In addition, the foreclosure rate on mortgages is negligible. In a recent survey conducted by the Mortgage Bankers Association, it was reported that the percentage of the mortgages placed in foreclosure at the end of the first quarter of 1975 was 0.01%.

Foreclosure rate (percentage of outstanding mortgages):

Regions	%
B.C.	0.0
Prairies	0.0
Ontario	0.01
Quebec	0.02
Atlantic Provinces	0.03
Average	0.01

Mortgages provide a monthly stream of repayments, rather than the lump-sum repayment of most bonds. This stream makes it possible to "dollar average." This facility can be of tremendous importance in compensating investors during large changes in capital market conditions. But despite these improvements in the mortgage contract, mortgages have continued to trade at a traditional premium of one or two percentage points above bonds and have continued to be a residual claimant on capital market funds. The illiquidity aspect obviously has been the *major* handicap.

What are the benefits of a secondary mortgage market?

1. The development of a secondary market, where existing mortgages can be exchanged, improves the marketability of mortgages. With improved marketability, more funds are attracted to mortgages, thus reducing the spread in yield between mortgages and other investments. Though it's possible that mortgages can continue to be a relatively high-yield investment, some trade-off between yield and marketability is likely to occur.

2. A market makes lenders less hesitant to make commitments during periods of changing financial condition. For example, in February 1975, when interest rates started inching down a notch or two, a number of lenders were hesitant to make mortgage loans, because they believed the decline was a temporary phenomenon. They regarded it as imprudent to make five-year loans in February at 10½% when they might obtain 12% in August. A centralized exchange minimizes this hesitancy and par-

tially removes the need to gamble on the time horizons of interest rate reversals.

3. It helps lenders or investors in adjusting their asset-mix to reduce any portfolio imbalance. For anyone administering an asset-portfolio, active trading of those assets should be part of exercising good management. An astute bond manager doesn't buy a 20-year 10½% bond because he's confident the interest-rate changes that will occur over the life of the bond will conform to his perceptions. Rather, he buys because of his short-term outlook and the attractive switching opportunities an actively traded secondary bond market affords him. He's been denied this facility with mortgages.

4. A tangential benefit is that institutional managers with a proclivity for trading may find this characteristic a satisfying complement to their market flirtations.

5. A true secondary market also permits interest arbitrage — the simultaneous buying in one market and selling in another to take advantage of a price difference. This hasn't been possible, since the huge discount an investor has had to pay to dispose of a mortgage usually has been larger than the benefit he'd have secured from switching investments.

6. A market improves the competitiveness of the mortgage instrument by increasing the interest-rate responsiveness to market situations. Mortgage yields have tended to show smaller amplitudes in their fluctuations than other yields taken from changes on outstanding issues. Put another way, a secondary market, by maintaining a continuous market in both the buying and selling side, allows yields to respond more closely to market situations.

7. It provides an alternative for yield-conscious savers. When interest rates begin to rise, as a result of monetary restraint, there's usually a disintermediation of funds from trust companies. Yield-conscious savers withdraw their funds and put them in direct market investments. A centralized exchange may attract some of these financial flows, with the result that these funds are retained in the mortgage market.

8. An improvement of the climate in which mortgages operate can be expected. The improved public relations and education attached to the establishment of a centralized exchange can increase people's appreciation and knowledge of the product.

9. It offers the private investor a greater security in trading on a *national* basis. The informal market has had a bias for localized operations.

Given all the incentives of a true mortgage exchange, who supplies the additional funds? Chartered banks have been lending mortgage money below their legal allowable maximum. The pension funds represent yet another area of increased availability. *The largest increment, however, could come from the personal sector.* Although the role of the private lender has been relegated to that of an approximate statistic at the national level, Ontario in a recent report on mortgages found that the personal sector financed 26.1% of the residential mortgage market. The figure in Quebec was 22.3%.

1973	Ontario	Quebec
		%
Personal sector..	26.1	22.3
Financial intermediaries.........................	56.8	55.3
Other corporations	10.5	4.5
Government agencies	6.6	17.9

Even though the mortgage product isn't part of the vocabulary of the average investor, there's a relatively high level of participation. Hence, we can assume that with improved liquidity and public relations, the commitment from this sector can be expanded. The personal sector's participation has originated mainly with notaries, lawyers and accountants whose professional involvement brings them in contact with the product. This leaves open the possibility that other professionals, as well as a number of yield-conscious savers, are likely to enter the market once a centralized exchange is established and recognized. An indication of this possibility can be gleaned from the bias shown by savers to mortgage funds attached to RRSPs. For example, in 1974 the net assets at market value of Royal Trust's non-mortgage funds was $103,456,153, while its mortgage fund totaled $318,870,140.

One of the major handicaps to the establishment of a mortgage exchange is the fragmentation of the mortgage market. The large size and non-homogeneous nature of the residential property market create a variety of situations in the mortgage contract. Thus each mortgage loan is affected by factors such as the location and quality of the security offered, the age and type of the contract, and the credit-worthiness of the borrower. In addition, the multiplicity of mortgage contracts — conventional, NHA, loans on new properties, loans on existing properties — exacerbate the problem of organizing an exchange.

Further complications involve the compounding period, the schedule of repayment, and the rate of interest. The contract rate on a mortgage might be 10%, but the effective rate might be much higher due to price variables such as legal fees, finder's fee, and placement fees. But despite the individualistic nature of the mortgage contract, there are enough similarities that mortgages can be classified to facilitate trading.

The major factors to take into account are the dollar size of the contract, the risk involved, the interest rate, and the date of renewal. One way to structure this in a true mortgage exchange is to set up symbols involving these main elements. The dollar size of the contract is designated 10 for each $10,000. So, a $25,000 mortgage is 25. The bid and ask price are similarly designated. For example, 24½ asking price is $24,500, while a 24¼ bid price is $24,250. The nature of the risk involved is symbolized by letters. "A" represents insured mortgages. The insurance feature eliminates the need to analyze the borrower or the nature of the security offered. "B" represents bellwether mortgages that aren't insured. "C" mortgages — with a fairly high debt/equity ratio. And "D" mortgages — highly speculative. The interest rate stated on the contract is used as part of the symbol, with the age of the contract providing the broad classifications under which mortgages are recorded. (See the table on page 163.)

Though sufficient characteristics exist to classify mortgages, the immensity and diversity of the residential mortgage market creates organizational and structural problems for the exchange. The magnitude of this problem emerges when one realizes that the total number of actively traded companies listed on all Canadian exchanges is 2,144. On the other hand, there are nearly seven million homes in Canada.

The problem, however, isn't as insurmountable as the figures initially suggest. In 1974, there were only 109,909 properties sold through Multiple Listing Service across Canada. The year before, there were 106,311. In 1974, the number of mortgage loans given by financial institutions, including NHA — on both new and existing stock — was 249,651. Of this total, Ontario alone had 100,132. Quebec got 50,237 and Vancouver 37,461. Though this statistical information is no indicator of the actual number of potential transactions on an exchange, it does indicate that the market base isn't too unwieldy for a number of regional exchanges.

Another major problem originates with the lack of security identification. When someone intends buying Bell Canada bonds or Cadillac Fairview stock, it's possible to rationalize investment intentions by analyzing financial statements. Thus one is able to move from the general — say, utilities or real estate — to the specific. With mortgages, we remain with the general. Mitigating elements, however, are the existence of credit reports on the mortgagor, the usually conservative appraisal of real property markets, the increasing number of properties that are being insured, and the fact that property in Canada has been benefiting from the underlying inflationary trend.

With these features, mortgages can almost be traded like government paper. The secondary mortgage market not only can provide a reasonably even flow of new funds for housing, but it can open an interesting field for personal investors and savers who've been wary of it in the past.

Secondary mortgage market listings

Type of mortgage	Renewal date	Asking price	Bid price 1 year old	Effective yield to maturity
35A12...........	June 80	34¼	34	11¾

This is a $35,000, 12% mortgage with negligible risk because of the insurance feature. The asking price is $34,250, the bid price is $34,000. The yield to maturity is 11¾.

Type of mortgage	Renewal date	Asking price	Bid price 1 year old	Effective yield to maturity
24B11	Dec. 79	23	22¾	12

This is a $24,000, 11% mortgage with little foreseeable capital loss, due to the creditworthiness of the borrower or the value of the property. However, it is not insured.

Type of mortgage	Renewal date	Asking price	Bid price 1 year old	Effective yield to maturity
10D12..........	Feb. 80	8⅞	8½	14

A highly speculative, $10,000, 12% mortgage.

Type of mortgage	Renewal date	Asking price	Bid price 2 years old	Effective yield to maturity
70A10½........	Dec. 78	68	67½	12
50C10..........	Sept. 78	47	46	13

Type of mortgage	Renewal date	Asking price	Bid price 3 years old	Effective yield to maturity
30C9.............	May 77	26	25	11

Type of mortgage	Renewal date	Asking price	Bid price 4 years old	Effective yield to maturity
25D9.............	Mar. 77	20	18½	12½

Type of mortgage	Renewal date	Asking price	Bid price 5 years old	Effective yield to maturity
17B8½	Feb. 76	14	12	7½

All mortgages based on five-year term, 25-year amortization. These are figures for illustrative purposes and are not necessarily mathematically correct.

Other money management books from Financial Post Books:

Your Money: How to Make the Most of It, by Robert H. Catherwood.

Your Guide to Investing for Bigger Profits, by C. Warren Goldring.

Life Insurance & The Businessman, edited by Robert H. Catherwood.

Real Estate for Profit, by Robert H. Catherwood.

Running Your Own Business, by the Institute of Chartered Accountants of Ontario.

Also from Financial Post Books:

Takeover
by Philip Mathias; the inside story of a massive take-over, the 22 days of risk and decision that created the world's largest newsprint empire, Abitibi-Price.

The Risk Takers
by Alexander Ross; a lively look at real-life contemporary Canadian entrepreneurs and how they built their own businesses from dreams.

Galt, U.S.A.
by Robert L. Perry; an award-winning study of the "American presence" and foreign investment in Canada, seen through the eyes of the people of a small Canadian city.

Women in Business
by James E. Bennett and Pierre M. Loewe; the first popular probe into the dangers and implications of the shocking treatment of women in Canadian organizations.

Accounting for Inflation
edited by Michael O. Alexander, CA; a basic work for anyone trying to understand the failure of traditional accounting methods to cope with the ravages of inflation.